To

Meg

From

Mike & Yvonne

Merry Christmas.
2012

PROVERBS PRAYERS

Praying the
Wisdom of Proverbs
Into Your Life
Every Day

JOHN MASON

summerside
PRESS

summerside
PRESS

Summerside Press™
Minneapolis, MN 55378
www.summersidepress.com

Proverbs Prayers

© 2012 by John Mason
ISBN 978-1-60936-169-3

Stock or custom editions of Summerside Press titles may be purchased in bulk
for educational, business, ministry, fundraising, or sales promotional use. For
information, please e-mail specialmarkets@summersidepress.com.

Cover and interior designed by Thinkpen Design | thinkpendesign.com

*Summerside Press™ is an inspirational publisher offering fresh,
irresistible books to uplift the heart and engage the mind.*

Printed in Canada.

DEDICATION

It's easy to dedicate this book to the greatest family on earth.

To my wife, Linda, thanks for being my best friend and for laughing with me every day.

To Michelle, for being someone who always has a song in her heart.

To Greg, for his peaceful persistence.

To Mike, for his unique creativity.

To Dave, for his boundless energy.

To my parents, Chet and Lorene Mason, for their love, prayers, and support.

The beginning of wisdom is: Acquire wisdom; and with all your acquiring, get understanding.

INTRODUCTION

Think about it…if you could pick one spiritual goal for your life, what would it be? For many people it would include praying and reading their Bible every day, especially the book of Proverbs. Several years ago, when I was reading through the Bible, I felt the Lord challenge me to pray the words I had just read. When I did, something happened. The words came alive to me. As I did this over time, His Word became clearer and I began to see changes in my life—good changes!

Proverbs Prayers is a book written to help you every day. God can change you when you open your life to Him. When you read each proverb and pray the corresponding prayer, you will be asking the Lord to cause every promise and principle from that chapter to come alive in your life. As you do, I believe that God is going to show you some things you've never seen before. You will pray about things that you may have been unaware of or have been avoiding (i.e., anger, lust, your words, etc.). And at the end of thirty-one days, wisdom will be your friend.

Thank you for the privilege of sharing God's Word with you. Get ready to grow!

1

¹ The proverbs of Solomon the son of David, king of Israel: ² To know wisdom and instruction, to discern the sayings of understanding, ³ To receive instruction in wise behavior, righteousness, justice and equity; ⁴ To give prudence to the naive, to the youth knowledge and discretion, ⁵ A wise man will hear and increase in learning, and a man of understanding will acquire wise counsel, ⁶ To understand a proverb and a figure, the words of the wise and their riddles. ⁷ The fear of the LORD is the beginning of knowledge; fools despise wisdom and instruction. ⁸ Hear, my son, your father's instruction and do not forsake your mother's teaching; ⁹ Indeed, they are a graceful wreath to your head and ornaments about your neck. ¹⁰ My son, if sinners entice you, do not consent. ¹¹ If they say, "Come with us, let us lie in wait for blood, let us ambush the innocent without cause; ¹² Let us swallow them alive like Sheol, even whole, as those who go down to the pit; ¹³ We will find all kinds of precious wealth, we will fill our houses with spoil; ¹⁴ Throw in your lot with us, we shall all have one purse," ¹⁵ My son, do not walk in the way with them. Keep your feet from their path, ¹⁶ For their feet run to evil and they hasten to shed blood. ¹⁷ Indeed, it is useless to spread the baited net in the sight of any bird; ¹⁸ But they lie in wait for their own blood; they ambush their own lives. ¹⁹ So are the ways of everyone

who gains by violence; it takes away the life of its possessors. [20] Wisdom shouts in the street, she lifts her voice in the square; [21] At the head of the noisy streets she cries out; at the entrance of the gates in the city she utters her sayings: [22] "How long, O naive ones, will you love being simple-minded? And scoffers delight themselves in scoffing and fools hate knowledge? [23] Turn to my reproof, behold, I will pour out my spirit on you; I will make my words known to you. [24] Because I called and you refused, I stretched out my hand and no one paid attention; [25] And you neglected all my counsel and did not want my reproof; [26] I will also laugh at your calamity; I will mock when your dread comes, [27] When your dread comes like a storm and your calamity comes like a whirlwind, when distress and anguish come upon you. [28] Then they will call on me, but I will not answer; they will seek me diligently but they will not find me, [29] Because they hated knowledge and did not choose the fear of the LORD. [30] They would not accept my counsel, they spurned all my reproof. [31] So they shall eat of the fruit of their own way and be satiated with their own devices. [32] For the waywardness of the naive will kill them, and the complacency of fools will destroy them. [33] But he who listens to me shall live securely and will be at ease from the dread of evil."

Proverbs 1

PRAYER

Thank You, Lord, for Your wisdom in Proverbs. I am forever appreciative of the life-giving instruction and understanding this precious book brings to me. I know You want it to be an indispensable part of my life so I ask You to help me hear Your Words today. As I do, I will increase in learning.

Help me remember my mother and father's wise words. Lead me to receive wise advice and have an appropriate reverence for You in my life. When I do, You will entrust supernatural information to me. Help me avoid being foolish by rejecting Your wisdom and instruction.

Open my eyes to see when sinners cross my path simply to tempt me. If that happens, I choose to immediately take a stand and say no. When they talk persuasively and promise all kinds of success to me, I trust You will stand by me in opposition to them. I don't want to become one of them. Direct my steps and keep me far away from these harmful associations. Keep my feet from heading in the wrong direction.

Lord, are there sinners in my life right now who are trying to persuade me to do the wrong thing? Please show me who they are. I need Your help to keep me free from their influence.

Help me to avoid greed because this kind of selfishness takes away the life that is inside me. Instead, let me conquer greed by becoming a giver.

Is there any area of greed in my life today, Lord? Please show me. Send opportunities for me to give today. I ask to be sensitive to hear what wisdom has to say. I don't want to be foolish by hating knowledge. It is my desire to heed Your warning and to change through wisdom's lessons. Pour Your Spirit on me and show me Your Words.

Lord, I choose to listen to Your wisdom today. I will not disdain or disregard it. As I do, I trust You will keep me from tragedy and terror. Because I fear You and love knowledge, I am confident You will hear me when I call to You. When I seek You diligently, I will find You. What a privilege it is to follow You and Your wisdom.

Father, help me listen clearly to Your wisdom so I can dwell safely and securely, without fear of evil.

2

¹ My son, if you will receive my words and treasure my commandments within you, ² Make your ear attentive to wisdom, incline your heart to understanding; ³ For if you cry for discernment, lift your voice for understanding; ⁴ If you seek her as silver and search for her as for hidden treasures; ⁵ Then you will discern the fear of the LORD and discover the knowledge of God. ⁶ For the LORD gives wisdom; from His mouth come knowledge and understanding. ⁷ He stores up sound wisdom for the upright; He is a shield to those who walk in integrity, ⁸ Guarding the paths of justice, and He preserves the way of His godly ones. ⁹ Then you will discern righteousness and justice and equity and every good course. ¹⁰ For wisdom will enter your heart and knowledge will be pleasant to your soul; ¹¹ Discretion will guard you, understanding will watch over you, ¹² To deliver you from the way of evil, from the man who speaks perverse things; ¹³ From those who leave the paths of uprightness to walk in the ways of darkness;¹⁴ Who delight in doing evil and rejoice in the perversity of evil; ¹⁵ Whose paths are crooked, and who are devious in their ways; ¹⁶ To deliver you from the strange woman, from the adulteress who flatters with her words; ¹⁷ That leaves the companion of her youth and forgets the covenant of her God; ¹⁸ For her house sinks down to death and her tracks lead to the dead; ¹⁹ None who go to her

return again, nor do they reach the paths of life. [20] So you will walk in the way of good men and keep to the paths of the righteous. [21] For the upright will live in the land and the blameless will remain in it; [22] But the wicked will be cut off from the land and the treacherous will be uprooted from it.

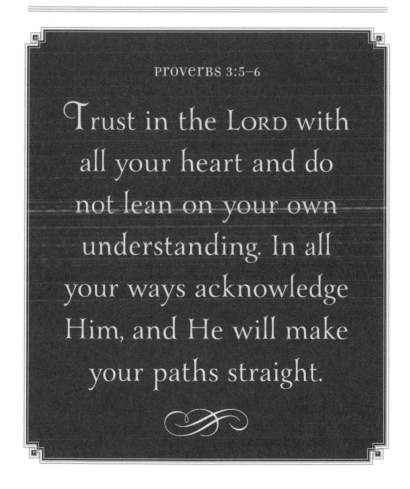

proverbs 3:5–6

Trust in the LORD with all your heart and do not lean on your own understanding. In all your ways acknowledge Him, and He will make your paths straight.

proverbs 2

PRAYER

Lord, Your words are so precious to me that I enthusiastically receive them and determine to hide them deep within my heart. Help me to hear Your wisdom and open my heart to understanding. From my innermost being, I yearn for knowledge. I lift up my voice to ask for understanding.

Today, I decide to seek after Your wisdom. I focus my attention and energies to search for it like a person searches for hidden treasure. When I do this, I know You will help me understand how to honor You. In what areas do You want me to increase in wisdom today?

Lord, I thank You for giving Your wisdom, knowledge, and understanding to me. Show me how to walk with integrity. As I do, I know You are going to protect me. Today, I firmly embrace Your sound wisdom as I do my best to live the righteous life You've called me to live.

Thank You for keeping me on the path of wise judgment by showing me the right way to go. I am grateful for Your promise of saving me and preserving me as I do what You want me to do. Help me to hear wisdom and let it penetrate deep within my heart. When I do, that knowledge will become pleasant to my soul.

Lord, save me from immoral people, particularly those who have enticing and flattering words. Help me be a person of discretion and understanding because those character traits protect me. Remove any evil person who comes into my life, especially those who speak and say things against You.

With the help of Your insight and strength, I'm not going to have relationships with people who don't want to follow You, who choose evil and are happy about it. Thank You for delivering me from them.

Lord, help me walk with good people and stay on the right path today.

3

¹ My son, do not forget my teaching, but let your heart keep my commandments; ² For length of days and years of life and peace they will add to you. ³ Do not let kindness and truth leave you; bind them around your neck, write them on the tablet of your heart. ⁴ So you will find favor and good repute in the sight of God and man. ⁵ Trust in the LORD with all your heart and do not lean on your own understanding. ⁶ In all your ways acknowledge Him, and He will make your paths straight. ⁷ Do not be wise in your own eyes; fear the LORD and turn away from evil. ⁸ It will be healing to your body and refreshment to your bones. ⁹ Honor the LORD from your wealth and from the first of all your produce; ¹⁰ So your barns will be filled with plenty and your vats will overflow with new wine. ¹¹ My son, do not reject the discipline of the LORD or loathe His reproof, ¹² For whom the LORD loves He reproves, even as a father corrects the son in whom he delights. ¹³ How blessed is the man who finds wisdom and the man who gains understanding. ¹⁴ For her profit is better than the profit of silver and her gain better than fine gold. ¹⁵ She is more precious than jewels; and nothing you desire compares with her. ¹⁶ Long life is in her right hand; in her left hand are riches and honor. ¹⁷ Her ways are pleasant ways and all her paths are peace. ¹⁸ She is a tree of life to those who take hold of her, and happy are all who hold

her fast. [19] The LORD by wisdom founded the earth, by understanding He established the heavens. [20] By His knowledge the deeps were broken up and the skies drip with dew. [21] My son, let them not vanish from your sight; keep sound wisdom and discretion, [22] So they will be life to your soul and adornment to your neck. [23] Then you will walk in your way securely and your foot will not stumble. [24] When you lie down, you will not be afraid; when you lie down, your sleep will be sweet. [25] Do not be afraid of sudden fear nor of the onslaught of the wicked when it comes; [26] For the LORD will be your confidence and will keep your foot from being caught. [27] Do not withhold good from those to whom it is due, when it is in your power to do it. [28] Do not say to your neighbor, "Go, and come back, and tomorrow I will give it," when you have it with you. [29] Do not devise harm against your neighbor, while he lives securely beside you. [30] Do not contend with a man without cause, if he has done you no harm. [31] Do not envy a man of violence and do not choose any of his ways. [32] For the devious are an abomination to the LORD; but He is intimate with the upright. [33] The curse of the LORD is on the house of the wicked, but He blesses the dwelling of the righteous. [34] Though He scoffs at the scoffers, yet He gives grace to the afflicted. [35] The wise will inherit honor, but fools display dishonor.

PROVERBS 3

PRAYER

ord, I open my heart again today to obey all Your commandments because they give me a long, peaceful life. I will never forget Your Word. I ask for Your help in letting mercy and truth dominate my life so I can find favor and understanding with You and with others.

Today, I choose to trust You with all of my heart and not depend on my own understanding. Help me to acknowledge You in everything; then I will know exactly which way to go. Lord, I choose to reject the desire of my ego. I don't want to be wise in my own eyes, so help me to resist pride. Instead, I want to fear You and stay away from evil. When I do, health and strength will come into my life.

Today, I choose to honor You with my possessions. I choose to give You the best part of any increase that comes into my life. As I do, You will bless my life to overflowing.

From this moment on, I'm not going to reject any corrections, realignment, or adjustment that You bring to me. And Lord, because I am Your child, I won't grow weary of them, even if You have to correct me over and over again. Is there anything You would like to correct in me today, Lord? Change me, Lord. I open my life to Your reorganization.

I thank You that as I find wisdom and gain understanding, I will be a happier person. Assist me in understanding the value of wisdom and seeing why it is greater than rubies, silver, or fine gold. Your wisdom will lengthen my days while bringing marvelous results.

Help me keep wisdom and discretion as an integral part of my life. As I do, Lord, I know they will bring life to my soul and grace to my life.

Lord, I sincerely ask You today to send opportunities for me to do good to others, especially when I can do something to make a genuine difference. Keep me from plotting and cultivating evil against others who have put their trust and confidence in me. Remove envy from my life, especially toward those who are deceitful and greedy. Help me to stay free from any of these ways.

And thank You, Lord, that my house is not cursed because of wickedness. Your blessing comes on my household as I try to walk justly before You. I pray that I will have a humble attitude today. As I do, I know You will give me grace. I thank You that honor comes to those who walk in Your wisdom.

When I go to bed tonight, keep me from being afraid of anything so I will sleep peacefully. Thank You for delivering me from any unexpected fear of being destroyed. You are my confidence, and You will keep me safe.

4

¹ Hear, O sons, the instruction of a father, and give attention that you may gain understanding, ² For I give you sound teaching; do not abandon my instruction. ³ When I was a son to my father, tender and the only son in the sight of my mother, ⁴ Then he taught me and said to me, "Let your heart hold fast my words; keep my commandments and live; ⁵ Acquire wisdom! Acquire understanding! Do not forget nor turn away from the words of my mouth. ⁶ Do not forsake her, and she will guard you; love her, and she will watch over you. ⁷ The beginning of wisdom is: Acquire wisdom; and with all your acquiring, get understanding. ⁸ Prize her, and she will exalt you; she will honor you if you embrace her. ⁹ She will place on your head a garland of grace; she will present you with a crown of beauty." ¹⁰ Hear, my son, and accept my sayings and the years of your life will be many. ¹¹ I have directed you in the way of wisdom; I have led you in upright paths. ¹² When you walk, your steps will not be impeded; and if you run, you will not stumble. ¹³ Take hold of instruction; do not let go. Guard her, for she is your life. ¹⁴ Do not enter the path of the wicked and do not proceed in the way of evil men. ¹⁵ Avoid it, do not pass by it; turn away from it and pass on. ¹⁶ For they cannot sleep unless they do evil; and they are robbed of sleep unless they make someone stumble. ¹⁷ For they eat the bread

of wickedness and drink the wine of violence. ¹⁸ But the path of the righteous is like the light of dawn, that shines brighter and brighter until the full day. ¹⁹ The way of the wicked is like darkness; they do not know over what they stumble. ²⁰ My son, give attention to my words; incline your ear to my sayings. ²¹ Do not let them depart from your sight; keep them in the midst of your heart. ²² For they are life to those who find them and health to all their body. ²³ Watch over your heart with all diligence, for from it flow the springs of life. ²⁴ Put away from you a deceitful mouth and put devious speech far from you. ²⁵ Let your eyes look directly ahead and let your gaze be fixed straight in front of you. ²⁶ Watch the path of your feet and all your ways will be established. ²⁷ Do not turn to the right nor to the left; turn your foot from evil.

Proverbs 4

PRAYER

Lord, I choose to pursue Your wisdom and understanding today. They are valuable to me. Help me to never abandon wisdom because it will protect and promote me. I want my love for wisdom, to grow, so I have decided to make wisdom a priority in my life. And along with wisdom, Lord help me to gain understanding of Your Word and obey it.

It's wonderful to know that when You are directing my steps on the right path, my steps are not hindered. I can run and not stumble.

Without hesitation, I choose to receive Your instructions and not let go for any reason. As I receive and hear Your sayings, I will live longer. They bring life to me!

Steer me away from the path of the wicked. Instead, I will turn from it and go in the opposite direction. I choose to avoid it completely. Lord, help me to see today that the path of the just is like a shining light. The longer I stay on it the brighter it gets, but the path of the unethical is dark. So help me, Lord, to follow Your Word. Fine-tune my ears to hear what You have to say.

Because I love Your Word so much, I promise to read and receive it deep within my heart today. Doing so will bring life and health to my whole being.

Help me to guard my heart at all times because it affects every area of my life. Lord, keep me from saying deceptive and vulgar words.

Are there words I say that are profane or deceitful? Lord, if there are, please deliver me from them. Keep me focused on what is right. Remove every distraction from my life. Help me to think seriously about the path I have chosen. Direct me so I can place all of my steps in the right direction. Today, I am determined to stick to Your path and stay away from evil.

5

¹ My son, give attention to my wisdom, incline your ear to my understanding; ² That you may observe discretion and your lips may reserve knowledge. ³ For the lips of an adulteress drip honey and smoother than oil is her speech; ⁴ But in the end she is bitter as wormwood, sharp as a two-edged sword. ⁵ Her feet go down to death, her steps take hold of Sheol. ⁶ She does not ponder the path of life; her ways are unstable, she does not know it. ⁷ Now then, my sons, listen to me and do not depart from the words of my mouth. ⁸ Keep your way far from her and do not go near the door of her house, ⁹ Or you will give your vigor to others and your years to the cruel one; ¹⁰ And strangers will be filled with your strength and your hard-earned goods will go to the house of an alien; ¹¹ And you groan at your final end, when your flesh and your body are consumed; ¹² And you say, "How I have hated instruction! And my heart spurned reproof! ¹³ I have not listened to the voice of my teachers, nor inclined my ear to my instructors! ¹⁴ I was almost in utter ruin in the midst of the assembly and congregation." ¹⁵ Drink water from your own cistern and fresh water from your own well. ¹⁶ Should your springs be dispersed abroad, streams of water in the streets? ¹⁷ Let them be yours alone and not for strangers with you. ¹⁸ Let your fountain be blessed, and rejoice in the wife of your youth. ¹⁹ As a loving hind and a graceful doe, let

her breasts satisfy you at all times; be exhilarated always with her love. [20] For why should you, my son, be exhilarated with an adulteress and embrace the bosom of a foreigner? [21] For the ways of a man are before the eyes of the Lord, and He watches all his paths. [22] His own iniquities will capture the wicked, and he will be held with the cords of his sin. [23] He will die for lack of instruction, and in the greatness of his folly he will go astray.

PRAYER

ord, I choose today to pay close attention to wisdom and listen intently to understanding. By doing so, I will exercise discretion, and what I say will be wise and full of knowledge. In what areas do I need to grow in wisdom and understanding?

Keep me from sexually immoral people. Their words may be smooth, but their ways are more destructive than a two-edged sword. The path they want to take me down only leads to death and hell. I decide today to not follow that path. I won't even consider choosing their ways. Instead, I will run from them and stay away from where they are. For I know, Lord, that if I ever go that way, I can lose my wealth and bring shame into my life. The credit for my hard work will go to others, and years of productivity will be lost. Therefore, I choose to rejoice with the wife (husband) of my youth. Thank You for her (his) love. I celebrate her (him), and choose to be sexually faithful to only her (him).

Lord, if immoral people are trying to influence my life today, I pray that You would show me who they are and deliver me from their influence.

I know that everywhere I go and in everything I do, You see what is going on. You are watching me closely. You are weighing and considering my daily choices.

Lord, I don't want to be like the immoral man who ends up doomed by his own sins, trapped in what he has done. I want to live a life free in You. Thank You for Your instruction and truth.

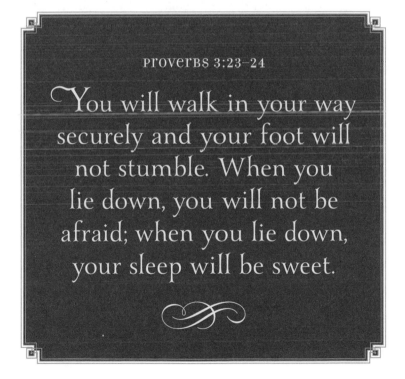

PROVERBS 3:23–24

You will walk in your way securely and your foot will not stumble. When you lie down, you will not be afraid; when you lie down, your sleep will be sweet.

6

¹ My son, if you have become surety for your neighbor, have given a pledge for a stranger, ² If you have been snared with the words of your mouth, have been caught with the words of your mouth, ³ Do this then, my son, and deliver yourself; since you have come into the hand of your neighbor, go, humble yourself, and importune your neighbor. ⁴ Give no sleep to your eyes, nor slumber to your eyelids; ⁵ Deliver yourself like a gazelle from the hunter's hand and like a bird from the hand of the fowler. ⁶ Go to the ant, O sluggard, observe her ways and be wise, ⁷ Which, having no chief, officer or ruler, ⁸ Prepares her food in the summer and gathers her provision in the harvest. ⁹ How long will you lie down, O sluggard? When will you arise from your sleep? ¹⁰ "A little sleep, a little slumber, a little folding of the hands to rest"— ¹¹ Your poverty will come in like a vagabond and your need like an armed man. ¹² A worthless person, a wicked man, is the one who walks with a perverse mouth, ¹³ Who winks with his eyes, who signals with his feet, who points with his fingers; ¹⁴ Who with perversity in his heart continually devises evil, who spreads strife. ¹⁵ Therefore his calamity will come suddenly; instantly he will be broken and there will be no healing. ¹⁶ There are six things which the LORD hates, yes, seven which are an abomination to Him: ¹⁷ Haughty eyes, a lying tongue, and hands that shed innocent blood, ¹⁸ A

heart that devises wicked plans, feet that run rapidly to evil, ¹⁹ A false witness who utters lies, and one who spreads strife among brothers. ²⁰ My son, observe the commandment of your father and do not forsake the teaching of your mother; ²¹ Bind them continually on your heart; tie them around your neck. ²² When you walk about, they will guide you; when you sleep, they will watch over you; and when you awake, they will talk to you. ²³ For the commandment is a lamp and the teaching is light; and reproofs for discipline are the way of life ²⁴ To keep you from the evil woman, from the smooth tongue of the adulteress. ²⁵ Do not desire her beauty in your heart, nor let her capture you with her eyelids. ²⁶ For on account of a harlot one is reduced to a loaf of bread, and an adulteress hunts for the precious life. ²⁷ Can a man take fire in his bosom and his clothes not be burned? ²⁸ Or can a man walk on hot coals and his feet not be scorched? ²⁹ So is the one who goes in to his neighbor's wife; whoever touches her will not go unpunished. ³⁰ Men do not despise a thief if he steals to satisfy himself when he is hungry; ³¹ But when he is found, he must repay sevenfold; he must give all the substance of his house. ³² The one who commits adultery with a woman is lacking sense; he who would destroy himself does it. ³³ Wounds and disgrace he will find, and his reproach will not be blotted out. ³⁴ For jealousy enrages a man, and he will not spare in the day of vengeance. ³⁵ He will not accept any ransom, nor will he be satisfied though you give many gifts.

proverbs 6

PRAYER

Lord, lead me so I can be wise in my financial matters today. Keep me from being a guarantor on a loan for another person. Keep me away from this kind of trouble. I don't want to be trapped by making a foolish agreement. Help me today to consider what I say because I know that I can become literally snared by what I say.

Thank You for creating the ant, Lord. Because You have presented ants as an example, I want to learn from their ways and become wise. They work hard and do things in the right season. When they need something, their resources are always there because they are diligent in their work. Deliver me from becoming a lazy person.

Are there any areas of laziness in my life, Lord? Please reveal them to me. I don't want to be lazy because if I am, poverty can creep up on me like a robber and steal from me. Help me to be diligent today.

Open my eyes to see wrong associations in my life. Remove and keep them away from me. I don't want corrupt, immoral, and ungodly people hanging around in my life. Deliver me from liars and those who are deceptive in everything they do.

Keep me from people who are thinking up new ways to take advantage of others and from those who stir up trouble everywhere they go. Show me who these people are so I can avoid them. Thank You that I will not find myself in a hopeless situation full of trouble because of bad influences in my life.

Free me from these things that You hate: a proud look, a lying tongue, hands that take advantage of the innocent, a heart that invents immoral ideas, feet that hurry to sin, a person who lies to cause strife among people who care about each other.

Lord, I honor my parents' instruction because they can help and guide me. I thank You for Your Holy Spirit who helps me to be an honest person and gives me discernment when others are telling lies.

Deliver me today, Lord, from any lust I have toward others. Help me turn my eyes away from any destructive temptation. I choose to not allow lust into my heart. I know that this kind of behavior is disasterous because it destroys my soul.

Lord, Your Word is a lamp, and Your law is a light in my life. Thank You for keeping me from evil people and safe from their crafty words.

7

¹ My son, keep my words and treasure my commandments within you. ² Keep my commandments and live, and my teaching as the apple of your eye. ³ Bind them on your fingers; write them on the tablet of your heart. ⁴ Say to wisdom, "You are my sister," and call understanding your intimate friend; ⁵ That they may keep you from an adulteress, from the foreigner who flatters with her words. ⁶ For at the window of my house I looked out through my lattice, ⁷ And I saw among the naive, and discerned among the youths a young man lacking sense, ⁸ Passing through the street near her corner; and he takes the way to her house, ⁹ In the twilight, in the evening, in the middle of the night and in the darkness. ¹⁰ And behold, a woman comes to meet him, dressed as a harlot and cunning of heart. ¹¹ She is boisterous and rebellious, her feet do not remain at home; ¹² She is now in the streets, now in the squares, and lurks by every corner. ¹³ So she seizes him and kisses him and with a brazen face she says to him: ¹⁴ "I was due to offer peace offerings; today I have paid my vows. ¹⁵ Therefore I have come out to meet you, to seek your presence earnestly, and I have found you. ¹⁶ I have spread my couch with coverings, with colored linens of Egypt. ¹⁷ I have sprinkled my bed with myrrh, aloes and cinnamon. ¹⁸ Come, let us drink our fill of love until morning; let us delight ourselves with caresses. ¹⁹ For my husband is

not at home, he has gone on a long journey; [20] He has taken a bag of money with him, at the full moon he will come home." [21] With her many persuasions she entices him; with her flattering lips she seduces him. [22] Suddenly he follows her as an ox goes to the slaughter, or as one in fetters to the discipline of a fool, [23] Until an arrow pierces through his liver; as a bird hastens to the snare, so he does not know that it will cost him his life. [24] Now therefore, my sons, listen to me, and pay attention to the words of my mouth. [25] Do not let your heart turn aside to her ways, do not stray into her paths. [26] For many are the victims she has cast down, and numerous are all her slain. [27] Her house is the way to Sheol, descending to the chambers of death.

PRAYER

ord, I want to keep Your Word and capture Your commandments deep within my heart today. Doing this will free me to live a wonderful life. Your Word is the greatest thing I can imagine. It is the apple of my eye. It's so incredibly precious that I eagerly receive it in the deepest part of me. I choose to see, know, and understand everything from Your perspective.

Are there any areas of my life that I am viewing strictly from a human perspective instead of from Your point of view, Lord? Teach me what Your Word says about those areas so I can acquire Your perspective today.

Because I love wisdom so much I want to say, "Wisdom, you are my sister." I thankfully declare, "Understanding is my close friend!" That way wisdom and understanding will keep me from the influences of bad men and women. In fact, I'm going to use Your wisdom to help keep me from evil people and their flattery every day.

I know that no person is immune to temptation. So, I will remember these important lessons from the story of the immoral woman. Like an oxen going to slaughter, many strong people have been taken down and ruined by yielding to temptations. Therefore, I will resist the lure of association with sexually immoral people, especially when they speak enticing words. I will turn from them and listen to Your Word instead of letting my heart be pulled toward them. The road they want me to travel along only leads to hell and death. I choose holiness today. I say no to temptation and lust.

Thank You, Lord, for caring so much for me!

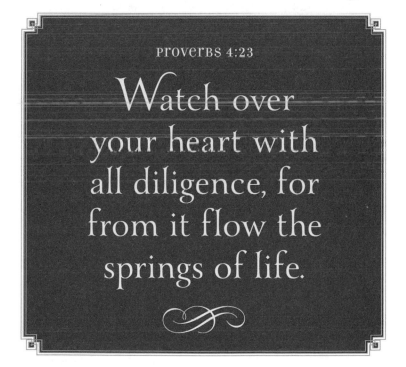

proverbs 4:23

Watch over your heart with all diligence, for from it flow the springs of life.

8

¹ Does not wisdom call, and understanding lift up her voice? ² On top of the heights beside the way, where the paths meet, she takes her stand; ³ Beside the gates, at the opening to the city, at the entrance of the doors, she cries out: ⁴ "To you, O men, I call, and my voice is to the sons of men. ⁵ O naive ones, understand prudence; and, O fools, understand wisdom. ⁶ Listen, for I will speak noble things; and the opening of my lips will reveal right things. ⁷ For my mouth will utter truth; and wickedness is an abomination to my lips. ⁸ All the utterances of my mouth are in righteousness; there is nothing crooked or perverted in them. ⁹ They are all straightforward to him who understands, and right to those who find knowledge. ¹⁰ Take my instruction and not silver, and knowledge rather than choicest gold. ¹¹ For wisdom is better than jewels; and all desirable things cannot compare with her. ¹² I, wisdom, dwell with prudence, and I find knowledge and discretion. ¹³ The fear of the LORD is to hate evil; pride and arrogance and the evil way and the perverted mouth, I hate. ¹⁴ Counsel is mine and sound wisdom; I am understanding, power is mine. ¹⁵ By me kings reign, and rulers decree justice. ¹⁶ By me princes rule, and nobles, all who judge rightly. ¹⁷ I love those who love me; and those who diligently seek me will find me. ¹⁸ Riches and honor are with me, enduring wealth and righteousness. ¹⁹ My fruit is better than gold,

even pure gold, and my yield better than choicest silver. ²⁰ I walk in the way of righteousness, in the midst of the paths of justice, ²¹ To endow those who love me with wealth, that I may fill their treasuries. ²² The LORD possessed me at the beginning of His way, before His works of old. ²³ From everlasting I was established, from the beginning, from the earliest times of the earth. ²⁴ When there were no depths I was brought forth, when there were no springs abounding with water. ²⁵ Before the mountains were settled, before the hills I was brought forth; ²⁶ While He had not yet made the earth and the fields, nor the first dust of the world. ²⁷ When He established the heavens, I was there, when He inscribed a circle on the face of the deep, ²⁸ When He made firm the skies above, when the springs of the deep became fixed, ²⁹ When He set for the sea its boundary so that the water would not transgress His command, when He marked out the foundations of the earth; ³⁰ Then I was beside Him, as a master workman; and I was daily His delight, rejoicing always before Him, ³¹ Rejoicing in the world, His earth, and having my delight in the sons of men. ³² Now therefore, O sons, listen to me, for blessed are they who keep my ways. ³³ Heed instruction and be wise, and do not neglect it. ³⁴ Blessed is the man who listens to me, watching daily at my gates, waiting at my doorposts. ³⁵ For he who finds me finds life and obtains favor from the Lord. ³⁶ But he who sins against me injures himself; all those who hate me love death."

PRAYER

Lord, open my ears to hear what wisdom and understanding have to say. Wisdom has important information for me and gives me common sense. When I look for wisdom, I can find it. It helps me to be a better leader, and it is infinitely more valuable than the best silver or gold. So, God, I ask for Your wisdom in every area of my life.

Today, I accept Your instruction and knowledge because it is valuable. Thank You that as I apply Your sound wisdom, it helps me make right decisions.

I choose to respect and fear You today. I choose to hate evil.

Create in me a loathing for pride, arrogance, corruption, deceit, evil ideas, and perverse words. Instead, help me embrace the good advice and the common sense of Your wisdom. It is because of wisdom's help that leaders are effective.

All those who love and search for wisdom will find more wisdom. So, please, lead me today to seek Your wisdom with all my heart.

Thank You that prosperity naturally follows Your wisdom and that healthy finances and honor can come into my life when I seek them. Abundance that lasts a long time comes as a result of Your wisdom. So, Lord, I want to receive all that You have for me. I trust in You.

The result of following Your way and judgment is better than having fine gold. Those who love and follow You are the wealthiest of all. When I hear Your instructions, I know I'll be wise.

Thank You, Lord, that Your wisdom has been here from the very beginning. It existed before the earth began. Yes, even when You established the heavens, wisdom was there. Wisdom was there when You marked out the foundations of the earth and was Your constant delight.

Is there any area of my life where I am refusing Your instruction today, Lord? I know that I'm blessed when I keep Your ways, so I choose to keep Your ways and receive Your blessings in my life.

9

¹ Wisdom has built her house, she has hewn out her seven pillars; ² She has prepared her food, she has mixed her wine; she has also set her table; ³ She has sent out her maidens, she calls from the tops of the heights of the city: ⁴ "Whoever is naive, let him turn in here!" To him who lacks understanding she says, ⁵ "Come, eat of my food and drink of the wine I have mixed. ⁶ Forsake your folly and live, and proceed in the way of understanding." ⁷ He who corrects a scoffer gets dishonor for himself, and he who reproves a wicked man gets insults for himself. ⁸ Do not reprove a scoffer, or he will hate you, reprove a wise man and he will love you. ⁹ Give instruction to a wise man and he will be still wiser, teach a righteous man and he will increase his learning. ¹⁰ The fear of the LORD is the beginning of wisdom, and the knowledge of the Holy One is understanding. ¹¹ For by me your days will be multiplied, and years of life will be added to you. ¹² If you are wise, you are wise for yourself, and if you scoff, you alone will bear it. ¹³ The woman of folly is boisterous, she is naive and knows nothing. ¹⁴ She sits at the doorway of her house, on a seat by the high places of the city, ¹⁵ Calling to those who pass by, who are making their paths straight: ¹⁶ "Whoever is naive, let him turn in here," and to him who lacks understanding she says, ¹⁷ "Stolen water is sweet; and

bread eaten in secret is pleasant." ¹⁸ But he does not know that the dead are there, that her guests are in the depths of Sheol.

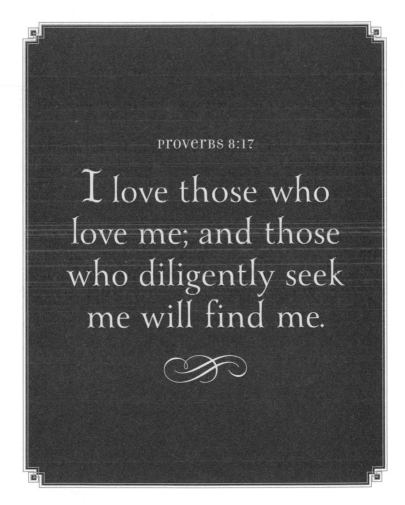

proverbs 8:17

I love those who love me; and those who diligently seek me will find me.

proverbs 9

PRAYER

ord, today I understand that wisdom is strong, calling me to come and receive. Your wisdom invites me to understand Your truth and ways. I have decided to pursue Your wisdom and truth.

I choose to turn my back on foolish things and live Your way. Is there any foolish thing I've allowed to come into my life? I ask You to remove it from me today and help me grow in spiritual things.

Today, I will not waste my time trying to correct someone who mocks others. Instead, let me become wise by receiving correction from a wise person. Thank You for opportunities to work with wise people and for the privilege of assisting them in becoming even wiser too. It's wonderful knowing that You bring every kind of understanding into my life as my knowledge of You grows. I want to know You more today, Lord.

Lord, I recognize that the fear of You is the beginning of wisdom, so I pray that my reverence of You will grow. I want to receive all of Your wisdom from today on. I know it makes every hour of my day more profitable and makes the years of my life abundant and fruitful. Wisdom is its own reward, and brings long life. Help me to receive Your direction today.

Help me steer clear of immoral people today. I will be alert to their sweet words, knowing that those who have been with them before are now in hell. Those kind of people don't bring life; they destroy the ignorant who blindly walk into their traps.

10

¹ The proverbs of Solomon. A wise son makes a father glad, but a foolish son is a grief to his mother. ² Ill-gotten gains do not profit, but righteousness delivers from death. ³ The Lord will not allow the righteous to hunger, but He will reject the craving of the wicked. ⁴ Poor is he who works with a negligent hand, but the hand of the diligent makes rich. ⁵ He who gathers in summer is a son who acts wisely, but he who sleeps in harvest is a son who acts shamefully. ⁶ Blessings are on the head of the righteous, but the mouth of the wicked conceals violence. ⁷ The memory of the righteous is blessed, but the name of the wicked will rot. ⁸ The wise of heart will receive commands, but a babbling fool will be ruined. ⁹ He who walks in integrity walks securely, but he who perverts his ways will be found out. ¹⁰ He who winks the eye causes trouble, and a babbling fool will be ruined. ¹¹ The mouth of the righteous is a fountain of life, but the mouth of the wicked conceals violence. ¹² Hatred stirs up strife, but love covers all transgressions. ¹³ On the lips of the discerning, wisdom is found, but a rod is for the back of him who lacks understanding. ¹⁴ Wise men store up knowledge, but with the mouth of the foolish, ruin is at hand. ¹⁵ The rich man's wealth is his fortress, the ruin of the poor is their poverty. ¹⁶ The wages of the righteous is life, the income of the wicked, punishment. ¹⁷ He is on the path of life who heeds

instruction, but he who ignores reproof goes astray. ¹⁸ He who
conceals hatred has lying lips, and he who spreads slander is a
fool. ¹⁹ When there are many words, transgression is unavoid-
able, but he who restrains his lips is wise. ²⁰ The tongue of the
righteous is as choice silver, the heart of the wicked is worth
little. ²¹ The lips of the righteous feed many, but fools die for
lack of understanding. ²² It is the blessing of the LORD that
makes rich, and He adds no sorrow to it. ²³ Doing wickedness
is like sport to a fool, and so is wisdom to a man of understanding. ²⁴ What the wicked fears will come upon him, but
the desire of the righteous will be granted. ²⁵ When the whirlwind passes, the wicked is no more, but the righteous has an
everlasting foundation. ²⁶ Like vinegar to the teeth and smoke
to the eyes, so is the lazy one to those who send him. ²⁷ The
fear of the LORD prolongs life, but the years of the wicked will
be shortened. ²⁸ The hope of the righteous is gladness, but the
expectation of the wicked perishes. ²⁹ The way of the LORD is
a stronghold to the upright, but ruin to the workers of iniquity. ³⁰ The righteous will never be shaken, but the wicked will
not dwell in the land. ³¹ The mouth of the righteous flows with
wisdom, but the perverted tongue will be cut out. ³² The lips of
the righteous bring forth what is acceptable, but the mouth of
the wicked what is perverted.

PRAYER

ord, thank You for showing me today that ill-gotten gain brings no lasting happiness. You always take care of those who do what is right. Help me to live in faithful obedience. Thank You for giving me the resolve to live steadfastly as a person who doesn't give up easily. Today I choose to be diligent. As I do, You will prosper me.

Help me find Your divine timing today so I can produce the greatest results at the most opportune time. I don't want to miss my hour of opportunity. I want to be in the middle of Your will.

I choose to be wise by receiving Your commandments and instructions. Help me understand that when I feel self-sufficient, I'm ripe for mistakes. Today I choose to walk in integrity and be confident as a result.

I'll not take sin lightly because I know that it will bring sorrow to my life. Remove any hatred I have toward others because this kind of attitude brings strife. And thank You, Lord, that love covers all sins.

Lord, help me to hold my tongue today. Help me to sincerely consider everything I say. Convict me if I'm inclined to pour out everything I know because continuous talking can lead to all kinds of problems.

Help me to be teachable in everything I do. That way, I'll be on the pathway to a productive and commendable life.

Lord, I know that only fools slander, so help me to not be a fool. If someone invites me to speak against another, keep me from talking too much or putting my foot in my mouth. Instead, let me be sensible, and stop talking. Please remind me to say good, life-giving words. When I do, my words will be more valuable than silver to those who hear them. Send opportunities to me to give good advice to help others.

Help me lead others to Your wisdom today. I want to be an example of Your truth with those who don't know You. Only Your blessings can bring prosperity without any negative results.

A fool's fun is doing mischief, but a wise person's fun is being uplifting. So help me today, Lord, to be wise. Teach me to be an excellent worker, never lazy, and a joy to those who work with me. Is there any way I can do a better job in my work today, Lord? How can I better treat those who work with me?

Lord, I see that the desires of good people will be met, but the wicked will lose everything. Your way brings strength to me, and by walking with You I'll live longer.

11

¹ A false balance is an abomination to the LORD, but a just weight is His delight. ² When pride comes, then comes dishonor, but with the humble is wisdom. ³ The integrity of the upright will guide them, but the crookedness of the treacherous will destroy them. ⁴ Riches do not profit in the day of wrath, but righteousness delivers from death. ⁵ The righteousness of the blameless will smooth his way, but the wicked will fall by his own wickedness. ⁶ The righteousness of the upright will deliver them, but the treacherous will be caught by their own greed. ⁷ When a wicked man dies, his expectation will perish, and the hope of strong men perishes. ⁸ The righteous is delivered from trouble, but the wicked takes his place. ⁹ With his mouth the godless man destroys his neighbor, but through knowledge the righteous will be delivered. ¹⁰ When it goes well with the righteous, the city rejoices, and when the wicked perish, there is joyful shouting. ¹¹ By the blessing of the upright a city is exalted, but by the mouth of the wicked it is torn down. ¹² He who despises his neighbor lacks sense, but a man of understanding keeps silent. ¹³ He who goes about as a talebearer reveals secrets, but he who is trustworthy conceals a matter. ¹⁴ Where there is no guidance the people fall, but in abundance of counselors there is victory. ¹⁵ He who is guarantor for a stranger will surely suffer for it, but he who hates

being a guarantor is secure. [16] A gracious woman attains honor, and ruthless men attain riches. [17] The merciful man does himself good, but the cruel man does himself harm. [18] The wicked earns deceptive wages, but he who sows righteousness gets a true reward. [19] He who is steadfast in righteousness will attain to life, and he who pursues evil will bring about his own death. [20] The perverse in heart are an abomination to the Lord, but the blameless in their walk are His delight. [21] Assuredly, the evil man will not go unpunished, but the descendants of the righteous will be delivered. [22] As a ring of gold in a swine's snout so is a beautiful woman who lacks discretion. [23] The desire of the righteous is only good, but the expectation of the wicked is wrath. [24] There is one who scatters, and yet increases all the more, and there is one who withholds what is justly due, and yet it results only in want. [25] The generous man will be prosperous, and he who waters will himself be watered. [26] He who withholds grain, the people will curse him, but blessing will be on the head of him who sells it. [27] He who diligently seeks good seeks favor, but he who seeks evil, evil will come to him. [28] He who trusts in his riches will fall, but the righteous will flourish like the green leaf. [29] He who troubles his own house will inherit wind, and the foolish will be servant to the wisehearted. [30] The fruit of the righteous is a tree of life, and he who is wise wins souls. [31] If the righteous will be rewarded in the earth, how much more the wicked and the sinner!

proverbs 11

PRAYER

choose to be ethical in everything I do today. I will not cheat. I want to be completely honest because I know that You delight in honesty. Remove pride from me so I am not a person who finishes in shame. I choose to be humble. The humble receive Your wisdom.

Lord, help me to be a person of integrity because integrity will guide me in the right way to go. Let me see that evil people are destroyed by their dishonesty. Help me gain the right perspective through knowing that only righteousness will count on judgment day and that riches will be of no help.

Help me to do what is right because righteousness will deliver me. I want to say only right words today because evil words destroy. So, Lord, help me watch my mouth. Keep me from quarreling with by neighbors. Help me to hold my tongue. Remove from me any compulsion to gossip or spread rumors.

I receive Your safety by surrounding myself with many counselors. I ask You to bring people into my life who are full of good advice so I will not fall.

Open my eyes to see that I should not offer to guarantee a debt for another person. Help me to understand that it's better to say no right away than to reap the consequences later. Is there a financial arrangement offered to me I should say no to?

Showing mercy to others nourishes my own soul. Help me to be merciful and not cruel, because those who are cruel to others destroy their own souls. Today, I want to sow righteousness so I can enjoy the harvest in my life forever.

Help me stay clear of the paths that lead to evil. Instead, I want to do the right thing and follow Your path for my life. I want to find life, not death.

Show me how to be a person of discretion and modesty in everything I say and do. Keep me from being stubborn in my heart toward You. I want to be a delight to You as an upright and good person.

Help me always to be a person who gives readily instead of one who holds on too tightly. I thank You that when I give, I become richer. If I hold on too tightly, I can lose everything. By helping others, I help myself. Lord, help me to become a liberal giver. Remove from me any faith I have in my own riches; misplaced trust will only bring failure.

As I trust in You today, I will grow and flourish. I will diligently seek good. When I do, I'll receive Your favor. I refuse to seek and follow after mischief because I don't want it to come looking for me.

Help me to be a godly person today, Lord, growing like a tree that gives out life-giving fruit. Help me win souls for You.

12

¹ Whoever loves discipline loves knowledge, but he who hates reproof is stupid. ² A good man will obtain favor from the LORD, but He will condemn a man who devises evil. ³ A man will not be established by wickedness, but the root of the righteous will not be moved. ⁴ An excellent wife is the crown of her husband, but she who shames him is like rottenness in his bones. ⁵ The thoughts of the righteous are just, but the counsels of the wicked are deceitful. ⁶ The words of the wicked lie in wait for blood, but the mouth of the upright will deliver them. ⁷ The wicked are overthrown and are no more, but the house of the righteous will stand. ⁸ A man will be praised according to his insight, but one of perverse mind will be despised. ⁹ Better is he who is lightly esteemed and has a servant than he who honors himself and lacks bread. ¹⁰ A righteous man has regard for the life of his animal, but even the compassion of the wicked is cruel. ¹¹ He who tills his land will have plenty of bread, but he who pursues worthless things lacks sense. ¹² The wicked man desires the booty of evil men, but the root of the righteous yields fruit. ¹³ An evil man is ensnared by the transgression of his lips, but the righteous will escape from trouble. ¹⁴ A man will be satisfied with good by the fruit of his words, and the deeds of a man's hands will return to him. ¹⁵ The way of a fool is right in his own eyes, but a wise man is he who listens

to counsel. ¹⁶ A fool's anger is known at once, but a prudent man conceals dishonor. ¹⁷ He who speaks truth tells what is right, but a false witness, deceit. ¹⁸ There is one who speaks rashly like the thrusts of a sword, but the tongue of the wise brings healing. ¹⁹ Truthful lips will be established forever, but a lying tongue is only for a moment. ²⁰ Deceit is in the heart of those who devise evil, but counselors of peace have joy. ²¹ No harm befalls the righteous, but the wicked are filled with trouble. ²² Lying lips are an abomination to the LORD, but those who deal faithfully are His delight. ²³ A prudent man conceals knowledge, but the heart of fools proclaims folly. ²⁴ The hand of the diligent will rule, but the slack hand will be put to forced labor. ²⁵ Anxiety in a man's heart weighs it down, but a good word makes it glad. ²⁶ The righteous is a guide to his neighbor, but the way of the wicked leads them astray. ²⁷ A lazy man does not roast his prey, but the precious possession of a man is diligence. ²⁸ In the way of righteousness is life, and in its pathway there is no death.

proverbs 12

PRAYER

 each me to love instruction and knowledge today, Lord. When I turn my back on correction I look stupid. Don't let me do that.

Thank You that when I seek to be a good person Your favor blesses my life. Thank You for showing me that a life lived only in righteousness has a solid foundation. Help me understand that wickedness and evil will never bring real success.

Fill my mind with right and honest thoughts today. Protect me from the counsel of wicked people who are full of lies and deceit. Deliver me from a perverse heart. Fill my life with Your wisdom.

I choose to work hard and to provide. I know that hard work brings blessing and that only a fool wastes time. Lord, are there any areas in my life I can work on more diligently today?

Help me to say the right thing. Keep me from lies that get me into trouble. Instead, let my integrity honestly speak for itself and deliver me.

Lord, please don't let me foolishly think that I'll never need good advice. Help me see the error in trying to be right in my own eyes. Rather, let me receive good counsel. Help me listen to others and gain wisdom.

Help me today, Lord, to not be quick-tempered. I don't want anger to dominate my life. Instead, I choose to be thoughtful, always keeping my cool when trouble is all around. I will speak the truth and do the right thing.

Help me to avoid saying things that might hurt other people. I decide now to say good words that bring others blessing, healing, and peace.

Thank You, Father, that Your truth always outlives a lie. A lie may win in the short run, but it never lasts long because truth endures forever. Remove from me any area of deceit and thoughts of evil so I will not be an abomination to You. Instead, let me be a person of peace and joy who is full of plans for good. Help me to deal truly and purposefully in everything I do today. No matter what the circumstances, help me keep my promises and my word. I want to be Your delight.

Help me to live a godly life so I will have no need to fear death. I want to work hard and smart today; I want to be a diligent person. Father, please remove any area of laziness, heaviness, or anxiousness in my heart.

13

¹ A wise son accepts his father's discipline, but a scoffer does not listen to rebuke. ² From the fruit of a man's mouth he enjoys good, but the desire of the treacherous is violence. ³ The one who guards his mouth preserves his life; the one who opens wide his lips comes to ruin. ⁴ The soul of the sluggard craves and gets nothing, but the soul of the diligent is made fat. ⁵ A righteous man hates falsehood, but a wicked man acts disgustingly and shamefully. ⁶ Righteousness guards the one whose way is blameless, but wickedness subverts the sinner. ⁷ There is one who pretends to be rich, but has nothing; another pretends to be poor, but has great wealth. ⁸ The ransom of a man's life is his wealth, but the poor hears no rebuke. ⁹ The light of the righteous rejoices, but the lamp of the wicked goes out. ¹⁰ Through insolence comes nothing but strife, but wisdom is with those who receive counsel. ¹¹ Wealth obtained by fraud dwindles, but the one who gathers by labor increases it. ¹² Hope deferred makes the heart sick, but desire fulfilled is a tree of life. ¹³ The one who despises the word will be in debt to it, but the one who fears the commandment will be rewarded. ¹⁴ The teaching of the wise is a fountain of life, to turn aside from the snares of death. ¹⁵ Good understanding produces favor, but the way of the treacherous is hard. ¹⁶ Every prudent man acts with knowledge, but a fool displays folly. ¹⁷ A wicked messenger falls into

adversity, but a faithful envoy brings healing. [18] Poverty and shame will come to him who neglects discipline, but he who regards reproof will be honored. [19] Desire realized is sweet to the soul, but it is an abomination to fools to turn away from evil. [20] He who walks with wise men will be wise, but the companion of fools will suffer harm. [21] Adversity pursues sinners, but the righteous will be rewarded with prosperity. [22] A good man leaves an inheritance to his children's children, and the wealth of the sinner is stored up for the righteous. [23] Abundant food is in the fallow ground of the poor, but it is swept away by injustice. [24] He who withholds his rod hates his son, but he who loves him disciplines him diligently. [25] The righteous has enough to satisfy his appetite, but the stomach of the wicked is in need.

PRAYER

hank You, Lord, for helping me say the right words. When they come out of my mouth, they produce good fruit in my life. Remove from me an argumentative or hurtful vocabulary. Show me today when to keep my mouth shut and how to control my tongue. Keep me from verbally reacting to others. Thank You that when I control my tongue, You will keep my life safe and guard me from destruction.

Remove slothfulness and laziness from my life, Lord. Don't let mediocrity rule my life. Today, I choose to be a diligent person, working hard and showing increase in my life. Thank You for promising to help me prosper when I live my life Your way.

I want to be a righteous person the rest of my life. I have chosen to avoid lies and inaccuracies. Keep me from following evil or harming myself by my own wickedness. Remove pride from my life today because it only leads to arguments, strife, and contention.

Lord, in what areas of my life does pride have a grip? Please show me. Help me to be humble and accept good counsel this week so I will become wiser.

Keep me from situations that indefinitely postpone what I'm hoping for. They make my heart sick. Let me understand today that there is no greater reward than to hold fast and true to Your will and Your Word. I choose to never disregard or reject Your Word because doing so would result in personal destruction. Instead, I will honor Your commandments, obey them, and succeed.

Today, I will actively pursue and take the advice of wise people. As I do, that wisdom will refresh me and become a fountain of life to me, keeping me aware of and away from pitfalls and problems that lie ahead.

Lord, teach me to be thoughtful in everything I do. Direct me in how to think and plan ahead. Help me to receive good instruction in every area of my life. I am determined to listen to and accept the right kind of correction today. As I do, You will bring honor into my life and remove poverty and shame.

Lord, I thank You for right associations in my life. I only want to walk with wise people, because they help me become wiser and wiser. Let me recognize and disconnect from any foolish companions in my life.

Help me to improve my parenting skills today, Lord. Never let me be afraid of disciplining my children. Thank You for the love I show them through faithful correction.

14

¹ The wise woman builds her house, but the foolish tears it down with her own hands. ² He who walks in his uprightness fears the LORD, but he who is devious in his ways despises Him. ³ In the mouth of the foolish is a rod for his back, but the lips of the wise will protect them. ⁴ Where no oxen are, the manger is clean, but much revenue comes by the strength of the ox. ⁵ A trustworthy witness will not lie, but a false witness utters lies. ⁶ A scoffer seeks wisdom and finds none, but knowledge is easy to one who has understanding. ⁷ Leave the presence of a fool, or you will not discern words of knowledge. ⁸ The wisdom of the sensible is to understand his way, but the foolishness of fools is deceit. ⁹ Fools mock at sin, but among the upright there is good will. ¹⁰ The heart knows its own bitterness, and a stranger does not share its joy. ¹¹ The house of the wicked will be destroyed, but the tent of the upright will flourish. ¹² There is a way which seems right to a man, but its end is the way of death. ¹³ Even in laughter the heart may be in pain, and the end of joy may be grief. ¹⁴ The backslider in heart will have his fill of his own ways, but a good man will be satisfied with his. ¹⁵ The naive believes everything, but the sensible man considers his steps. ¹⁶ A wise man is cautious and turns away from evil, but a fool is arrogant and careless. ¹⁷ A quick-tempered man acts foolishly, and a man of evil devices

is hated. ¹⁸ The naive inherit foolishness, but the sensible are crowned with knowledge. ¹⁹ The evil will bow down before the good, and the wicked at the gates of the righteous. ²⁰ The poor is hated even by his neighbor, but those who love the rich are many. ²¹ He who despises his neighbor sins, but happy is he who is gracious to the poor. ²² Will they not go astray who devise evil? But kindness and truth will be to those who devise good. ²³ In all labor there is profit, but mere talk leads only to poverty. ²⁴ The crown of the wise is their riches, but the folly of fools is foolishness. ²⁵ A truthful witness saves lives, but he who utters lies is treacherous. ²⁶ In the fear of the LORD there is strong confidence, and his children will have refuge. ²⁷ The fear of the LORD is a fountain of life, that one may avoid the snares of death. ²⁸ In a multitude of people is a king's glory, but in the dearth of people is a prince's ruin. ²⁹ He who is slow to anger has great understanding, but he who is quick-tempered exalts folly. ³⁰ A tranquil heart is life to the body, but passion is rottenness to the bones. ³¹ He who oppresses the poor taunts his Maker, but he who is gracious to the needy honors Him. ³² The wicked is thrust down by his wrongdoing, but the righteous has a refuge when he dies. ³³ Wisdom rests in the heart of one who has understanding, but in the hearts of fools it is made known. ³⁴ Righteousness exalts a nation, but sin is a disgrace to any people. ³⁵ The king's favor is toward a servant who acts wisely, but his anger is toward him who acts shamefully.

proverbs 14

PRAYER

Lord, I choose to walk right before You and honor You today. Deliver me from perversity which brings disgrace to You. Remove pride from me so my words won't become foolish. I want to say only wise things and receive Your protection.

Teach me today to be a truthful person. Remove any insults, criticism, or skepticism I may harbor toward others. Instead, let me be a person of understanding. Allow knowledge to come easily to me. Help me discern the truth when I am in the presence of foolish people. Let me be sensitive to what others say so I'll know whether or not I should be around them.

Help me to be prudent and to carefully consider every choice I make. Help me recognize any area of dishonesty in my life. I want to be honest and triumphant, instead of being deceitful and defeated. Keep me from being wise in my own eyes and choosing my own ways. Direct me along Your path only.

Lord, if there is something I believe that I shouldn't, please reveal it to me so I can change. I want to be wise by being cautious and avoiding danger. I don't want to believe everything I hear or see. Help me to consider every step I take.

Today, I choose to depart from every kind of evil. Help me to avoid the foolishness of going full steam ahead, trusting in the confidence of my own actions. Help me to stay free from anger, so I won't end up doing unwise things. Help me to not look down on others or ignore them. Instead, help me see with Your eyes and show Your mercy to the poor. Reveal new ways for me to help them. When I follow Your ways, happiness will come into my life.

I refuse any temptation to plot evil against anyone. Instead, I plan to do good. When I do, mercy and truth will come into my life. Lord, help me to be a doer, not just a talker. If I only talk about situations, nothing happens. But if I work at it, there is a reward. Help me to say and do the right things today, Lord. That is the best way to help other people.

Keep me from participating in foolishness. Protect me from the destructiveness of envy, I don't want to be jealous of others. Create in me a peaceful heart that is life-giving.

Help me to never oppress the poor. Instead, teach me how to show them mercy. Lord, what can I do now to help those less fortunate than me?

Because of my reverence for You, Lord, I have deep strength and strong confidence. Your certainty provides a place of refuge and a fountain of life to me. Thank You for Your blessing.

15

¹ A gentle answer turns away wrath, but a harsh word stirs up anger. ² The tongue of the wise makes knowledge acceptable, but the mouth of fools spouts folly. ³ The eyes of the LORD are in every place, watching the evil and the good. ⁴ A soothing tongue is a tree of life, but perversion in it crushes the spirit. ⁵ A fool rejects his father's discipline, but he who regards reproof is sensible. ⁶ Great wealth is in the house of the righteous, but trouble is in the income of the wicked. ⁷ The lips of the wise spread knowledge, but the hearts of fools are not so. ⁸ The sacrifice of the wicked is an abomination to the LORD, but the prayer of the upright is His delight. ⁹ The way of the wicked is an abomination to the LORD, but He loves one who pursues righteousness. ¹⁰ Grievous punishment is for him who forsakes the way; he who hates reproof will die. ¹¹ Sheol and Abaddon lie open before the LORD, how much more the hearts of men! ¹² A scoffer does not love one who reproves him, he will not go to the wise. ¹³ A joyful heart makes a cheerful face, but when the heart is sad, the spirit is broken. ¹⁴ The mind of the intelligent seeks knowledge, but the mouth of fools feeds on folly. ¹⁵ All the days of the afflicted are bad, but a cheerful heart has a continual feast. ¹⁶ Better is a little with the fear of the Lord than great treasure and turmoil with it. ¹⁷ Better is a dish of vegetables where love is than a fattened ox served with hatred.

¹⁸ A hot-tempered man stirs up strife, but the slow to anger calms a dispute. ¹⁹ The way of the lazy is as a hedge of thorns, but the path of the upright is a highway. ²⁰ A wise son makes a father glad, but a foolish man despises his mother. ²¹ Folly is joy to him who lacks sense, but a man of understanding walks straight. ²² Without consultation, plans are frustrated, but with many counselors they succeed. ²³ A man has joy in an apt answer, and how delightful is a timely word! ²⁴ The path of life leads upward for the wise that he may keep away from Sheol below. ²⁵ The LORD will tear down the house of the proud, but He will establish the boundary of the widow. ²⁶ Evil plans are an abomination to the LORD, but pleasant words are pure. ²⁷ He who profits illicitly troubles his own house, but he who hates bribes will live. ²⁸ The heart of the righteous ponders how to answer, but the mouth of the wicked pours out evil things. ²⁹ The LORD is far from the wicked, but He hears the prayer of the righteous. ³⁰ Bright eyes gladden the heart; good news puts fat on the bones. ³¹ He whose ear listens to the life-giving reproof will dwell among the wise. ³² He who neglects discipline despises himself, but he who listens to reproof acquires understanding. ³³ The fear of the LORD is the instruction for wisdom, and before honor comes humility.

PRAYER

ord, today, if I have an occasion to be angry, help me to give a peaceful response instead. Keep me from saying hard or hurtful words that stir up more anger.

I have decided to have an attitude that makes learning a joy. Keep me from talking too much and saying every foolish thing that comes into my head. I know You are everywhere, seeing and hearing everything that I do and say.

Remove from me any wickedness; I want to follow passionately after righteousness. Deliver me from being critical of others. Give me enduring joy inside and let it show in my smile. Thank You, Lord, for giving me so much to be thankful for! Take away any sorrow in my heart that makes me want to give up.

Today I will seek knowledge. I won't feed on foolishness. Help me to know, Lord, that a little combined with reverence for You is better than having great wealth and its trouble. Help me to be righteous and not slothful because the good way is like a smooth highway and the lazy person's path is full of snares.

I desire to be full of understanding and to live a holy life. I never want to lack Your wisdom. Please send people full of good advice into my life to help me reach my dreams and goals. In fact, through many advisors they will be established.

Help me to be a person who says the right things at the right time. Let me always choose Your way. Remove from my life any evil thoughts or ideas so I will not be an abomination to You.

Lord, have I had any thoughts lately that aren't pleasing to You? If so, I ask You to deliver me from that kind of thinking. Help me to be pure, speaking good and pleasant words.

Lord, guide me away from greed and keep me from troubling my own family. I will not take any bribes because they only lead to compromise. Help me to think before I respond to others. Remove from me any area of wickedness so You will stay close to me and hear my prayers.

Let my ears always be open to hear and receive the right kind of constructive criticism. Lord, keep me from refusing good and correct instruction. I know that if I accept wise criticism, I will gain understanding, and then You will bring more wise people into my life.

16

¹ The plans of the heart belong to man, but the answer of the tongue is from the LORD. ² All the ways of a man are clean in his own sight, but the LORD weighs the motives. ³ Commit your works to the LORD and your plans will be established. ⁴ The LORD has made everything for its own purpose, even the wicked for the day of evil. ⁵ Everyone who is proud in heart is an abomination to the LORD; assuredly, he will not be unpunished. ⁶ By loving kindness and truth iniquity is atoned for, and by the fear of the LORD one keeps away from evil. ⁷ When a man's ways are pleasing to the LORD, He makes even his enemies to be at peace with him. ⁸ Better is a little with righteousness than great income with injustice. ⁹ The mind of man plans his way, but the LORD directs his steps. ¹⁰ A divine decision is in the lips of the king; his mouth should not err in judgment. ¹¹ A just balance and scales belong to the LORD; all the weights of the bag are His concern. ¹² It is an abomination for kings to commit wicked acts, for a throne is established on righteousness. ¹³ Righteous lips are the delight of kings, and he who speaks right is loved. ¹⁴ The fury of a king is like messengers of death, but a wise man will appease it. ¹⁵ In the light of a king's face is life, and his favor is like a cloud with the spring rain. ¹⁶ How much better it is to get wisdom than gold! And to get understanding is to be chosen above silver. ¹⁷ The

highway of the upright is to depart from evil; he who watches his way preserves his life. ¹⁸ Pride goes before destruction, and a haughty spirit before stumbling. ¹⁹ It is better to be humble in spirit with the lowly than to divide the spoil with the proud. ²⁰ He who gives attention to the word will find good, and blessed is he who trusts in the LORD. ²¹ The wise in heart will be called understanding, and sweetness of speech increases persuasiveness. ²² Understanding is a fountain of life to one who has it, but the discipline of fools is folly. ²³ The heart of the wise instructs his mouth and adds persuasiveness to his lips. ²⁴ Pleasant words are a honeycomb, sweet to the soul and healing to the bones. ²⁵ There is a way which seems right to a man, but its end is the way of death. ²⁶ A worker's appetite works for him, for his hunger urges him on. ²⁷ A worthless man digs up evil, while his words are like scorching fire. ²⁸ A perverse man spreads strife, and a slanderer separates intimate friends. ²⁹ A man of violence entices his neighbor and leads him in a way that is not good. ³⁰ He who winks his eyes does so to devise perverse things; he who compresses his lips brings evil to pass. ³¹ A gray head is a crown of glory; it is found in the way of righteousness. ³² He who is slow to anger is better than the mighty, and he who rules his spirit, than he who captures a city. ³³ The lot is cast into the lap, but its every decision is from the LORD.

PRAYER

ord, thank You for showing me that You've made everything for Your own purposes. I ask You today for what is good, not just what looks good. I choose to commit all my work to You. Make my thinking clear and accurate.

Remove any pride from my heart today so I won't be an abomination to you or disgust You. Forgive me for any arrogance I have shown; I don't want to destroy my life. Rather, help me to have a humble spirit because it is better to be humble and poor than to be proud and rich.

I choose to respect and fear You today. Doing this keeps me safe and gives me protection from evil. I choose to have all my ways please You. You are able to keep my enemies at peace with me, and I thank You for that!

Lord, I have decided to gain Your wisdom and understanding because they are worth more than gold and fine silver. I will depend on You today to direct me when I make my plans. Help me to stay on the right path, far away from evil. Is the path I am presently taking the correct one? Please show me the right way to go. I know that when I take the godly path, I'll be safe and You will save my life.

I know, Lord, that anytime I trust in You, I will be happy and things will work out for the best. Therefore, I receive Your Word and choose to obey You today. Help me to have a wise heart and only use gracious, sweet words. When I do this, I will increase my understanding.

I want to let wisdom become a fountain of life to me. I want You to be a part of everything I do, so, Lord, I invite You into every area of my life. Keep me from choosing the path that I, by myself, think is right. I want Your direction because I don't know everything. I need Your help in avoiding disaster that can come through choices of my own.

Please keep me from digging up evil, sowing strife, and whispering gossip. I know this causes friendships to fall apart. I choose today to never gossip to my friends. Help me to rule my spirit today. Show me how to be slow tempered and exhibit self-control.

17

¹ Better is a dry morsel and quietness with it than a house full of feasting with strife. ² A servant who acts wisely will rule over a son who acts shamefully, and will share in the inheritance among brothers. ³ The refining pot is for silver and the furnace for gold, but the LORD tests hearts. ⁴ An evildoer listens to wicked lips; a liar pays attention to a destructive tongue. ⁵ He who mocks the poor taunts his Maker; he who rejoices at calamity will not go unpunished. ⁶ Grandchildren are the crown of old men, and the glory of sons is their fathers. ⁷ Excellent speech is not fitting for a fool, much less are lying lips to a prince. ⁸ A bribe is a charm in the sight of its owner; wherever he turns, he prospers. ⁹ He who conceals a transgression seeks love, but he who repeats a matter separates intimate friends. ¹⁰ A rebuke goes deeper into one who has understanding than a hundred blows into a fool. ¹¹ A rebellious man seeks only evil, so a cruel messenger will be sent against him. ¹² Let a man meet a bear robbed of her cubs, rather than a fool in his folly. ¹³ He who returns evil for good, evil will not depart from his house. ¹⁴ The beginning of strife is like letting out water, so abandon the quarrel before it breaks out. ¹⁵ He who justifies the wicked and he who condemns the righteous, both of them alike are an abomination to the LORD. ¹⁶ Why is there a price in the hand of a fool to buy wisdom, when he has no sense?

[17] A friend loves at all times, and a brother is born for adversity. [18] A man lacking in sense pledges and becomes guarantor in the presence of his neighbor. [19] He who loves transgression loves strife; he who raises his door seeks destruction. [20] He who has a crooked mind finds no good, and he who is perverted in his language falls into evil. [21] He who sires a fool does so to his sorrow, and the father of a fool has no joy. [22] A joyful heart is good medicine, but a broken spirit dries up the bones. [23] A wicked man receives a bribe from the bosom to pervert the ways of justice. [24] Wisdom is in the presence of the one who has understanding, but the eyes of a fool are on the ends of the earth. [25] A foolish son is a grief to his father and bitterness to her who bore him. [26] It is also not good to fine the righteous, nor to strike the noble for their uprightness. [27] He who restrains his words has knowledge, and he who has a cool spirit is a man of understanding. [28] Even a fool, when he keeps silent, is considered wise; when he closes his lips, he is considered prudent.

PRAYER

choose Your peace today rather than anything that would bring arguments and strife. I want to have a pure heart and a right spirit. Lord, are there any areas in my heart that aren't pure? Please purify my heart. Am I keeping a right spirit?

Keep me from believing and listening to lies. I am determined to not listen to those who are full of revenge. Remove liars from my life.

I choose to not rejoice over others' calamities or gloat over their misfortunes. I decide to never make fun of the poor which would bring dishonor to You.

Help me today, Lord, to forgive and forget others' mistakes, sins, and offenses. Never let me talk about these actions and bring a division among my friends. I choose to be a person of common sense and wisdom who is open to receive effective correction. I don't want to be rebellious and invite judgment into my life. Keep me from repaying evil for good so destruction will be kept from my family.

I choose to never start strife, because once it starts, it's hard to stop. Keep me, Lord, from justifying wicked things and wicked people. I don't want to take part in condemning the just and true. Keep me from having a deceitful heart that doesn't find any good. Remove from me any perverse words that lead to evil. I want to have a cheerful heart because it helps me like medicine helps sick people. Keep me from a broken spirit that makes me sick.

Lord, guide me in Your wisdom. I choose to make it my main pursuit. Show me how to use my words sparingly, with a calm spirit. Help me to keep my mouth shut when I'm not knowledgeable about something. By staying silent, I'll be considered perceptive and wise.

18

¹ He who separates himself seeks his own desire, he quarrels against all sound wisdom. ² A fool does not delight in understanding, but only in revealing his own mind. ³ When a wicked man comes, contempt also comes, and with dishonor comes scorn. ⁴ The words of a man's mouth are deep waters; the fountain of wisdom is a bubbling brook. ⁵ To show partiality to the wicked is not good, nor to thrust aside the righteous in judgment. ⁶ A fool's lips bring strife, and his mouth calls for blows. ⁷ A fool's mouth is his ruin, and his lips are the snare of his soul. ⁸ The words of a whisperer are like dainty morsels, and they go down into the innermost parts of the body. ⁹ He also who is slack in his work is brother to him who destroys. ¹⁰ The name of the LORD is a strong tower; the righteous runs into it and is safe. ¹¹ A rich man's wealth is his strong city, and like a high wall in his own imagination. ¹² Before destruction the heart of man is haughty, but humility goes before honor. ¹³ He who gives an answer before he hears, it is folly and shame to him. ¹⁴ The spirit of a man can endure his sickness, but as for a broken spirit who can bear it? ¹⁵ The mind of the prudent acquires knowledge, and the ear of the wise seeks knowledge. ¹⁶ A man's gift makes room for him and brings him before great men. ¹⁷ The first to plead his case seems right, until another comes and examines him. ¹⁸ The cast lot puts an end to strife

and decides between the mighty ones. ¹⁹ A brother offended is harder to be won than a strong city, and contentions are like the bars of a citadel. ²⁰ With the fruit of a man's mouth his stomach will be satisfied; he will be satisfied with the product of his lips. ²¹ Death and life are in the power of the tongue, and those who love it will eat its fruit. ²² He who finds a wife finds a good thing and obtains favor from the LORD. ²³ The poor man utters supplications, but the rich man answers roughly. ²⁴ A man of too many friends comes to ruin, but there is a friend who sticks closer than a brother.

proverbs 18:10

The name of the LORD is a strong tower; the righteous runs into it and is safe.

PRAYER

Lord, help me love those around me by sharing Your wisdom and love today. I don't want to be an isolated loner who only wants what I want and demands my own way. If I do that, I will find myself in opposition to every wise idea, thought, and decision.

I'll not foolishly reject understanding and only express my own thoughts today. Show me how to have deep wellsprings of wisdom flowing out of my life.

Lord, keep me from favoring wicked people and condemning those who do right. Keep me from saying words that can trap my soul and destroy me. Help me to understand that sin brings disgrace. Show me any rumors or gossip that I have been spreading or believing. Please keep me from tattling, gossiping, and spreading rumors.

Today, I choose to be diligent in everything I do. I believe that You are a fortress, a strong tower, One whom I can run to and be safe. Help me understand that being humble brings honor, while having an arrogant heart and being full of pride brings devastation.

Help me to hold my tongue and refrain from answering before knowing all the facts. Talking too soon will only bring mischief and shame to me. I choose to seek and acquire Your knowledge, always learning and listening. Enable me with a healthy, strong spirit that will sustain me in the middle of adversity. If a conflict arises, help me to be patient with others by taking the time to hear both sides of any problem. I know that only then will I be able to reach an accurate conclusion.

Keep me from offending other people, because it is almost impossible to win them back once I do. I know that words can either give life or take it. Help me today, Lord, to say good, positive, uplifting words that bring life. What are some life-giving words I can share with someone who needs them?

I thank You for helping me be (find) a good wife. I understand that I am (she is) a good thing and even bring(s) favor from You into my husband's (my) life.

I choose to be friendly to others so friends will be numerous in my life. And thank You again, Lord, that a real friend like You always sticks closer than a brother.

19

¹ Better is a poor man who walks in his integrity than he who is perverse in speech and is a fool. ² Also it is not good for a person to be without knowledge, and he who hurries his footsteps errs. ³ The foolishness of man ruins his way, and his heart rages against the LORD. ⁴ Wealth adds many friends, but a poor man is separated from his friend. ⁵ A false witness will not go unpunished, and he who tells lies will not escape. ⁶ Many will seek the favor of a generous man, and every man is a friend to him who gives gifts. ⁷ All the brothers of a poor man hate him; how much more do his friends abandon him! He pursues them with words, but they are gone. ⁸ He who gets wisdom loves his own soul; he who keeps understanding will find good. ⁹ A false witness will not go unpunished, and he who tells lies will perish. ¹⁰ Luxury is not fitting for a fool; much less for a slave to rule over princes. ¹¹ A man's discretion makes him slow to anger, and it is his glory to overlook a transgression. ¹² The king's wrath is like the roaring of a lion, but his favor is like dew on the grass. ¹³ A foolish son is destruction to his father, and the contentions of a wife are a constant dripping. ¹⁴ House and wealth are an inheritance from fathers, but a prudent wife is from the LORD. ¹⁵ Laziness casts into a deep sleep, and an idle man will suffer hunger. ¹⁶ He who keeps the commandment keeps his soul, but he who is careless of conduct will die.

[17] One who is gracious to a poor man lends to the LORD, and He will repay him for his good deed. [18] Discipline your son while there is hope, and do not desire his death. [19] A man of great anger will bear the penalty, for if you rescue him, you will only have to do it again. [20] Listen to counsel and accept discipline, that you may be wise the rest of your days. [21] Many plans are in a man's heart, but the counsel of the LORD will stand. [22] What is desirable in a man is his kindness, and it is better to be a poor man than a liar. [23] The fear of the LORD leads to life, so that one may sleep satisfied, untouched by evil. [24] The sluggard buries his hand in the dish, but will not even bring it back to his mouth. [25] Strike a scoffer and the naive may become shrewd, but reprove one who has understanding and he will gain knowledge. [26] He who assaults his father and drives his mother away is a shameful and disgraceful son. [27] Cease listening, my son, to discipline, and you will stray from the words of knowledge. [28] A rascally witness makes a mockery of justice, and the mouth of the wicked spreads iniquity [29] Judgments are prepared for scoffers, and blows for the back of fools.

PRAYER

ord, I decide to walk in integrity today. I don't want to say dishonest things like a fool. I want to be good, so I seek Your knowledge. Let me understand that haste makes waste.

I choose to not be foolish because it causes me to go down the wrong path. Help me always to be honest and avoid the punishment that comes to liars.

Today, I want to show that I love my own soul by acquiring wisdom. Help me to understand Your Word—to find what is good.

Assist me in showing good discretion today by being slow to anger. Help me be willing to overlook offenses done against me. I want to be a person who can forgive and forget. Are there people I need to forgive today, Lord? If there are, help me to forgive them.

Teach me to not be a negative, nagging person. Help me to be positive and sensible. And, Lord, please remove laziness and idleness from my life. I never want to become careless in my ways and invite my own destruction. I want to lead a diligent and productive life, so please help me to keep your commandments today. Thank You for preserving my mind, will, and emotions.

Show me if there is someone I can help today. Open my heart to show pity on the poor. I know that as I do, I will be giving to You. And You pay back what I give!

Lord, thank You for the opportunity to correct my children today while there is still hope. Keep me from setting my heart on their destruction. Stop me from becoming angry with them and suffering my own punishment as a result.

I thank You that even though I have many plans in my heart, it is Your direction that stands. It is Your purpose that always prevails. Help me to receive sound advice and good instruction that makes me wise in life. Deliver me from being a skeptic or a fool. I don't want to suffer the punishment of their critical ways.

Lord, I decide to be kind to everyone I know today. I choose to not mistreat my parents. Open me to receive all of Your counsel and instruction so I will live wisely and well. Let me understand that respect of You brings life, results in satisfaction, and keeps me from evil. Help me grow in Your wisdom and grace.

20

¹ Wine is a mocker, strong drink a brawler, and whoever is intoxicated by it is not wise. ² The terror of a king is like the growling of a lion; he who provokes him to anger forfeits his own life. ³ Keeping away from strife is an honor for a man, but any fool will quarrel. ⁴ The sluggard does not plow after the autumn, so he begs during the harvest and has nothing. ⁵ A plan in the heart of a man is like deep water, but a man of understanding draws it out. ⁶ Many a man proclaims his own loyalty, but who can find a trustworthy man? ⁷ A righteous man who walks in his integrity—how blessed are his sons after him. ⁸ A king who sits on the throne of justice disperses all evil with his eyes. ⁹ Who can say, "I have cleansed my heart, I am pure from my sin"? ¹⁰ Differing weights and differing measures, both of them are abominable to the LORD. ¹¹ It is by his deeds that a lad distinguishes himself if his conduct is pure and right. ¹² The hearing ear and the seeing eye, the Lord has made both of them. ¹³ Do not love sleep, or you will become poor; open your eyes, and you will be satisfied with food. ¹⁴ "Bad, bad," says the buyer, but when he goes his way, then he boasts. ¹⁵ There is gold, and an abundance of jewels; but the lips of knowledge are a more precious thing. ¹⁶ Take his garment when he becomes surety for a stranger; and for foreigners, hold him in pledge. ¹⁷ Bread obtained by falsehood

is sweet to a man, but afterward his mouth will be filled with gravel. ¹⁸ Prepare plans by consultation, and make war by wise guidance. ¹⁹ He who goes about as a slanderer reveals secrets, therefore do not associate with a gossip. ²⁰ He who curses his father or his mother, his lamp will go out in time of darkness. ²¹ An inheritance gained hurriedly at the beginning will not be blessed in the end. ²² Do not say, "I will repay evil"; wait for the LORD, and He will save you. ²³ Differing weights are an abomination to the LORD, and a false scale is not good. ²⁴ Man's steps are ordained by the LORD, how then can man understand his way? ²⁵ It is a trap for a man to say rashly, "It is holy!" and after the vows to make inquiry. ²⁶ A wise king winnows the wicked, and drives the threshing wheel over them. ²⁷ The spirit of man is the lamp of the LORD, searching all the innermost parts of his being. ²⁸ Loyalty and truth preserve the king, and he upholds his throne by righteousness. ²⁹ The glory of young men is their strength, and the honor of old men is their gray hair. ³⁰ Stripes that wound scour away evil, and strokes reach the innermost parts.

PRAYER

hank You, Lord, for keeping me from being led astray by alcohol and for guarding me from quarrels and fighting. Both are foolish activities and I'm grateful for Your presence that gives me strength to resist them.

I won't make excuses today for not completing my work on time, because when I eliminate them from my life, I receive a blessing.

Help me to not proclaim my own goodness today. Give me an opportunity to be a faithful friend. I ask You to help me be a righteous person who walks in integrity. As a result, my children will be blessed.

Lord, I know that I can never make my own heart clean and purify myself from sin. Only You can do that, so I ask You to forgive me of my sins and purify my heart today. Keep me from any area of deceit because You hate it. Help me understand that everyone, even a child, is known by the good or evil they do.

I do decide to not love sleep too much; instead I will energetically work to see fruitful results.

Lord, keep me from dishonesty and deception today. Thank You for showing me that any seeming sweetness of this disobedient strategy always results in a feeling as satisfying as a mouth filled with gravel.

Lead me to form my plans by seeking wise counsel, and help me to carry out advice by getting as much help as I possibly can. What plans do I have that need the guidance of wise counsel today, Lord? Is there anyone I should or shouldn't talk to about these plans? Please lead me to them.

Lord, please teach me to stay clear of gossips and flatterers. Show me who these people are and keep me separate from them. Also, help me to understand that quick gain at the start will not necessarily be blessed at the end. Help me to be patient and to trust Your timing.

I choose to not try to get even with others. Instead, I will trust in You and believe that You will justify and save me. Help me to not be deceitful, conniving, or untruthful in any relationship.

I trust You to direct my steps. Help me avoid the trap of making quick, rash commitments and promises, because I may not be able to get out of them later if I want to change my mind. Give me a clear understanding of how my spirit is like a lamp that You use to examine my innermost being. Help me to see how good correction can eradicate evil from my heart and life.

21

¹ The king's heart is like channels of water in the hand of the LORD; He turns it wherever He wishes. ² Every man's way is right in his own eyes, but the LORD weighs the hearts. ³ To do righteousness and justice is desired by the LORD more than sacrifice. ⁴ Haughty eyes and a proud heart, the lamp of the wicked, is sin. ⁵ The plans of the diligent lead surely to advantage, but everyone who is hasty comes surely to poverty. ⁶ The acquisition of treasures by a lying tongue is a fleeting vapor, the pursuit of death. ⁷ The violence of the wicked will drag them away, because they refuse to act with justice. ⁸ The way of a guilty man is crooked, but as for the pure, his conduct is upright. ⁹ It is better to live in a corner of a roof than in a house shared with a contentious woman. ¹⁰ The soul of the wicked desires evil; his neighbor finds no favor in his eyes. ¹¹ When the scoffer is punished, the naive becomes wise; but when the wise is instructed, he receives knowledge. ¹² The righteous one considers the house of the wicked, turning the wicked to ruin. ¹³ He who shuts his ear to the cry of the poor will also cry himself and not be answered. ¹⁴ A gift in secret subdues anger, and a bribe in the bosom, strong wrath. ¹⁵ The exercise of justice is joy for the righteous, but is terror to the workers of iniquity. ¹⁶ A man who wanders from the way of understanding will rest in the assembly of the dead. ¹⁷ He who loves pleasure

will become a poor man; he who loves wine and oil will not become rich. [18] The wicked is a ransom for the righteous, and the treacherous is in the place of the upright. [19] It is better to live in a desert land than with a contentious and vexing woman. [20] There is precious treasure and oil in the dwelling of the wise, but a foolish man swallows it up. [21] He who pursues righteousness and loyalty finds life, righteousness and honor. [22] A wise man scales the city of the mighty and brings down the stronghold in which they trust. [23] He who guards his mouth and his tongue, guards his soul from troubles. [24] "Proud," "Haughty," "Scoffer," are his names, who acts with insolent pride. [25] The desire of the sluggard puts him to death, for his hands refuse to work; [26] All day long he is craving, while the righteous gives and does not hold back. [27] The sacrifice of the wicked is an abomination, how much more when he brings it with evil intent! [28] A false witness will perish, but the man who listens to the truth will speak forever. [29] A wicked man displays a bold face, but as for the upright, he makes his way sure. [30] There is no wisdom and no understanding and no counsel against the LORD. [31] The horse is prepared for the day of battle, but victory belongs to the LORD.

PRAYER

ord, it's good to know that a leader's heart in Your hands is like a river of water that You can route wherever You wish.

Keep me from justifying every move I make, trying to look good in my own eyes today. I know You examine my heart and weigh my motives. I choose to be directed by You. I determine to do what is right with fairness. Keep me from having an arrogant attitude and a proud heart. I want to be diligent in everything I do, resulting in abundance coming into my life.

Because a lifestyle of hurry leads to poverty, help me today, Lord, to fully consider my decisions and pace of life. I choose to not give in to the temptation of dishonest gain because that kind of profit will never last. I will be fair and just to those around me.

Lord, remove any perverse ways from me. Instead, help me always do what's right with pure motives. Help me to not be a contentious, nagging person.

Open my ears to the cry and needs of the poor today, Lord. I know that those who disregard the poor will be ignored in their own time of need.

Help me understand how the love of too much pleasure and alcohol is unwise and leads to poverty. Lord, help me work hard and not try to get something for nothing. Help me follow goodness and mercy in order to find life, righteousness, and honor. Keep me focused and never let me wander from the way of understanding.

Help me to not long for what others have. Instead, I choose to do what is right and to be a liberal giver to others. Do I desire what someone else has today, Lord? Am I envious? If so, please show me.

I realize that a liar is always found out, so I determine always to speak truthfully. I choose to guard what I say, so I can keep my soul from trouble.

22

¹ A good name is to be more desired than great wealth, favor is better than silver and gold. ² The rich and the poor have a common bond, the LORD is the maker of them all. ³ The prudent sees the evil and hides himself, but the naive go on, and are punished for it. ⁴ The reward of humility and the fear of the LORD are riches, honor and life. ⁵ Thorns and snares are in the way of the perverse; he who guards himself will be far from them. ⁶ Train up a child in the way he should go, even when he is old he will not depart from it. ⁷ The rich rules over the poor, and the borrower becomes the lender's slave. ⁸ He who sows iniquity will reap vanity, and the rod of his fury will perish. ⁹ He who is generous will be blessed, for he gives some of his food to the poor. ¹⁰ Drive out the scoffer, and contention will go out, even strife and dishonor will cease. ¹¹ He who loves purity of heart and whose speech is gracious, the king is his friend. ¹² The eyes of the LORD preserve knowledge, but He overthrows the words of the treacherous man. ¹³ The sluggard says, "There is a lion outside; I will be killed in the streets!" ¹⁴ The mouth of an adulteress is a deep pit; he who is cursed of the LORD will fall into it. ¹⁵ Foolishness is bound up in the heart of a child; the rod of discipline will remove it far from him. ¹⁶ He who oppresses the poor to make more for himself or who gives to the rich, will only come to poverty. ¹⁷ Incline

your ear and hear the words of the wise, and apply your mind to my knowledge; [18] For it will be pleasant if you keep them within you, that they may be ready on your lips. [19] So that your trust may be in the LORD, I have taught you today, even you. [20] Have I not written to you excellent things of counsels and knowledge, [21] To make you know the certainty of the words of truth that you may correctly answer him who sent you? [22] Do not rob the poor because he is poor, or crush the afflicted at the gate; [23] For the LORD will plead their case and take the life of those who rob them. [24] Do not associate with a man given to anger; or go with a hot-tempered man, [25] Or you will learn his ways and find a snare for yourself. [26] Do not be among those who give pledges, among those who become guarantors for debts. [27] If you have nothing with which to pay, why should he take your bed from under you? [28] Do not move the ancient boundary which your fathers have set. [29] Do you see a man skilled in his work? He will stand before kings; he will not stand before obscure men.

proverbs 22

PRAYER

ord, I choose to have a good name today by displaying outstanding character. A good name is more valuable than great riches. I want to honor You. I ask You to help me be humble and to respect You today because when I do, You will bring riches, honor, and life. Help me to foresee evil and stay away from it.

Thank You that right action keeps punishment from my life. Deliver me from the trap of sinful things by guarding my soul from them.

Lord, help me to direct, lead, and train my children today in the right way to go. When I do, as they grow older, they'll continue to serve You. Is there any way I can lead and train my children better? Please reveal it to me. Give me a loving understanding of how the rod of discipline will drive foolishness and disrespect from them.

Today, help me to be honest, and as a result, I know You'll keep sorrow and destruction away from me. Keep me from anger that brings failure with it. Help me to show generosity to the poor and receive Your blessing in return. Remove troublemakers, skeptics, and critics from me. When they are gone from my life, strife, confusion, and contention will leave me alone.

I will guard my mind, will, and emotions today. Lord, help me to be pure hearted and to speak words of grace. As I do, leaders will become my friends. Lord, You guard knowledge and have nothing to do with dishonesty. Remove from my life any excuse that keeps me from doing the work I know I'm supposed to do.

I determine never to oppress the poor in order to increase my own wealth. I refuse to give to the rich in order to gain their favor because it only brings a worse poverty.

Lord, I know that it's a pleasant thing to keep Your knowledge and wisdom inside me, so I open my ears today to hear Your words of wisdom. I choose to diligently seek godly knowledge and to speak words full of wisdom. Doing this helps me to keep my trust in You.

Help me to never take advantage of or exploit the poor simply because they're poor. Show me how to help those who are afflicted and needy. I know You plead their case and come against the souls of those who take advantage of them. Help me to be sensitive today to those with great need.

Lord, keep me away from angry people. I don't want to become like them, which can become a snare for my soul. Help me to avoid making any pledges with others that could entangle me in their debt. I commit to being excellent, skillful, and hardworking at whatever I do today. In so doing, success and promotion will come to me and I will find myself associating with great people.

23

¹ When you sit down to dine with a ruler, consider carefully what is before you, ² And put a knife to your throat if you are a man of great appetite. ³ Do not desire his delicacies, for it is deceptive food. ⁴ Do not weary yourself to gain wealth, cease from your consideration of it. ⁵ When you set your eyes on it, it is gone. For wealth certainly makes itself wings like an eagle that flies toward the heavens. ⁶ Do not eat the bread of a selfish man, or desire his delicacies; ⁷ For as he thinks within himself, so he is. He says to you, "Eat and drink!" but his heart is not with you. ⁸ You will vomit up the morsel you have eaten, and waste your compliments. ⁹ Do not speak in the hearing of a fool, for he will despise the wisdom of your words. ¹⁰ Do not move the ancient boundary or go into the fields of the fatherless, ¹¹ For their Redeemer is strong; he will plead their case against you. ¹² Apply your heart to discipline and your ears to words of knowledge. ¹³ Do not hold back discipline from the child, although you strike him with the rod, he will not die. ¹⁴ You shall strike him with the rod and rescue his soul from Sheol. ¹⁵ My son, if your heart is wise, my own heart also will be glad; ¹⁶ And my inmost being will rejoice when your lips speak what is right. ¹⁷ Do not let your heart envy sinners, but live in the fear of the LORD always. ¹⁸ Surely there is a future, and your hope will not be cut off. ¹⁹ Listen, my son, and be

wise, and direct your heart in the way. ²⁰ Do not be with heavy drinkers of wine, or with gluttonous eaters of meat; ²¹ For the heavy drinker and the glutton will come to poverty, and drowsiness will clothe one with rags. ²² Listen to your father who begot you, and do not despise your mother when she is old. ²³ Buy truth, and do not sell it, get wisdom and instruction and understanding. ²⁴ The father of the righteous will greatly rejoice, and he who sires a wise son will be glad in him. ²⁵ Let your father and your mother be glad, and let her rejoice who gave birth to you. ²⁶ Give me your heart, my son, and let your eyes delight in my ways. ²⁷ For a harlot is a deep pit and an adulterous woman is a narrow well. ²⁸ Surely she lurks as a robber, and increases the faithless among men. ²⁹ Who has woe? Who has sorrow? Who has contentions? Who has complaining? Who has wounds without cause? Who has redness of eyes? ³⁰ Those who linger long over wine, those who go to taste mixed wine. ³¹ Do not look on the wine when it is red, when it sparkles in the cup, when it goes down smoothly; ³² At the last it bites like a serpent and stings like a viper ³³ Your eyes will see strange things and your mind will utter perverse things. ³⁴ And you will be like one who lies down in the middle of the sea, or like one who lies down on the top of a mast. ³⁵ "They struck me, but I did not become ill; they beat me, but I did not know it. When shall I awake? I will seek another drink."

proverbs 23

PRAYER

ord, when I have the opportunity to meet with influential people, let me consider who and what is before me. Help me exhibit good table manners and control over my appetite. I choose to not desire what they have in their lives because I know what they appear to have may not be exactly as it seems.

I will no longer depend on my own wisdom. Instead, I choose Your wisdom. I will show restraint, and I will avoid the empty activity of making money for money's sake. Riches are only temporary; they can disappear in the blink of an eye.

Keep me from associating with miserly, stingy people. They often have ulterior motives in their hearts and talking with them is just a waste of time. Keep me from throwing my words away by speaking to fools because they won't respect what I have to say. Thank You, Lord, for defending and protecting orphans. Show me how I can help them.

Open my heart and mind to instruction and correction. Are there some areas where You want me to receive further instruction today, Lord? What corrections do You have for me? Fine-tune my ears today to Your words of knowledge.

Today, I pray to have a wise heart and to speak the right things. If my children need correction, remind me of Your love so I can correct them properly, rescuing their souls from hell. I never want to become envious of sinners. Instead, I'll be zealous about my reverence for You. Because of You, I have a wonderful hope and future.

Lord, help me to listen to You and be wise, keeping my heart on the right path. Keep me away from people who drink too much alcohol and eat too much food. They end up in poverty, and I don't want to end up there with them.

Today, I determine to not be lazy. I will listen to my father and respect my mother. I will gain Your truth at any cost and never let go of it. I want to grab on to discernment, wisdom, instruction, and understanding.

Keep my heart and eyes pure. Remove all the immoral people who lie in wait for me. I know that relationships with them only bring sorrow, anguish, contention, and injuries into my life. Thank You for keeping me away from the influence of alcohol. It only hurts the drinker by making his mind unsteady and perverting his perspective on life. Why would I want to live like that?

Wonderful Counselor, thank You for hearing my prayer today. I praise You for Your wisdom. Thank You for giving it to me.

24

¹ Do not be envious of evil men, nor desire to be with them; ² For their minds devise violence, and their lips talk of trouble. ³ By wisdom a house is built, and by understanding it is established; ⁴ And by knowledge the rooms are filled with all precious and pleasant riches. ⁵ A wise man is strong, and a man of knowledge increases power. ⁶ For by wise guidance you will wage war, and in abundance of counselors there is victory. ⁷ Wisdom is too exalted for a fool, he does not open his mouth in the gate. ⁸ One who plans to do evil, men will call a schemer. ⁹ The devising of folly is sin, and the scoffer is an abomination to men. ¹⁰ If you are slack in the day of distress, your strength is limited. ¹¹ Deliver those who are being taken away to death, and those who are staggering to slaughter, oh hold them back. ¹² If you say, "See, we did not know this," does He not consider it who weighs the hearts? And does He not know it who keeps your soul? And will He not render to man according to his work? ¹³ My son, eat honey, for it is good, yes, the honey from the comb is sweet to your taste; ¹⁴ Know that wisdom is thus for your soul; if you find it, then there will be a future, and your hope will not be cut off. ¹⁵ Do not lie in wait, O wicked man, against the dwelling of the righteous; do not destroy his resting place; ¹⁶ For a righteous man falls seven times, and rises again, but the wicked stumble in time of calamity. ¹⁷ Do not

rejoice when your enemy falls, and do not let your heart be glad when he stumbles; [18] Or the LORD will see it and be displeased, and turn His anger away from him. [19] Do not fret because of evildoers or be envious of the wicked; [20] For there will be no future for the evil man; the lamp of the wicked will be put out. [21] My son, fear the LORD and the king; do not associate with those who are given to change, [22] For their calamity will rise suddenly, and who knows the ruin that comes from both of them? [23] These also are sayings of the wise. To show partiality in judgment is not good. [24] He who says to the wicked, "You are righteous," peoples will curse him, nations will abhor him; [25] But to those who rebuke the wicked will be delight, and a good blessing will come upon them. [26] He kisses the lips who gives a right answer. [27] Prepare your work outside and make it ready for yourself in the field; afterwards, then, build your house. [28] Do not be a witness against your neighbor without cause, and do not deceive with your lips. [29] Do not say, "Thus I shall do to him as he has done to me; I will render to the man according to his work." [30] I passed by the field of the sluggard and by the vineyard of the man lacking sense, [31] And behold, it was completely overgrown with thistles; its surface was covered with nettles, and its stone wall was broken down. [32] When I saw, I reflected upon it; I looked, and received instruction. [33] "A little sleep, a little slumber, a little folding of the hands to rest," [34] Then your poverty will come as a robber and your want like an armed man.

PRAYER

ord, keep me from becoming jealous of ungodly people today. Remove from me any desire to be with them or like them. Their hearts plot evil schemes and destruction. Their words are full of trouble. Are there people like that who are influencing my life? Lord, please show me who they are so I can discontinue my relationship with them.

Lord, today I see that it takes wisdom to build anything. By acquiring understanding, a right foundation for long-term growth is established. I see that by acquiring knowledge, overflowing abundance comes to me. Help me see that Your wisdom brings increasing strength and knowledge.

I promise to seek advice when conflicts with others arise. Thank You for safety that comes to me from listening to many good advisors. Remove foolishness and help me to not be critical or make fun of others.

Strengthen me so I don't give up in times of trouble. Help me to rescue those who are on the path of death and are moving blindly toward destruction. You know and weigh the motives of every person's heart. You know mine too, and You will reward all of us according to our deeds.

Your wisdom is like honey; it's so sweet to my soul. It assures me of a good future and that You will never abandon me.

If a righteous person falls down many times, he rises again and again. When the wicked are brought down by calamity and when my enemy falls or stumbles, help me to not be thrilled, Lord. If you see me having that attitude, remind me that You disapprove and that it will disrupt Your due course of judgment. Only You are worthy to avenge wrongdoers.

I don't care about the temporal success of wicked people because I know they have no future. The path they're on is a dead-end street, going the wrong way fast. Instead, I choose to fear, love, and reverence You, Lord.

Help me to choose good relationships. Give me Your wisdom to stay free from associations with rebellious people and deliver me from their evil plans. Help me avoid the calamity and disaster that comes through relationship with them.

Lord, help me to see injustice today. Don't let me call the wicked "good." Rather, give me the courage to expose the wicked for who they are. As a result, I will see blessings come into my life.

As long as I live, I have decided that an honest answer will always be my response. Keep me from speaking against my neighbor without cause or using my lips to deceive. I won't try to get even with anyone.

I don't want to live a life that is empty of understanding. Help me understand the lesson I can learn from the life of a lazy person. All around the lazy, things go unattended and fall apart. Poverty comes on them like a thief and their needs go unmet. Today, I decide to live a diligent life.

PROVERBS 16:3

Commit your
works to the LORD
and your plans will
be established.

25

¹ These also are proverbs of Solomon which the men of Hezekiah, king of Judah, transcribed. ² It is the glory of God to conceal a matter, but the glory of kings is to search out a matter. ³ As the heavens for height and the earth for depth, so the heart of kings is unsearchable. ⁴ Take away the dross from the silver, and there comes out a vessel for the smith; ⁵ Take away the wicked before the king, and his throne will be established in righteousness. ⁶ Do not claim honor in the presence of the king, and do not stand in the place of great men; ⁷ For it is better that it be said to you, "Come up here," than for you to be placed lower in the presence of the prince, whom your eyes have seen. ⁸ Do not go out hastily to argue your case; otherwise, what will you do in the end, when your neighbor humiliates you? ⁹ Argue your case with your neighbor, and do not reveal the secret of another, ¹⁰ Or he who hears it will reproach you, and the evil report about you will not pass away. ¹¹ Like apples of gold in settings of silver is a word spoken in right circumstances. ¹² Like an earring of gold and an ornament of fine gold is a wise reprover to a listening ear. ¹³ Like the cold of snow in the time of harvest is a faithful messenger to those who send him, for he refreshes the soul of his masters. ¹⁴ Like clouds and wind without rain is a man who boasts of his gifts falsely. ¹⁵ By forbearance a ruler may be persuaded, and a soft

tongue breaks the bone. [16] Have you found honey? Eat only what you need, that you not have it in excess and vomit it. [17] Let your foot rarely be in your neighbor's house, or he will become weary of you and hate you. [18] Like a club and a sword and a sharp arrow is a man who bears false witness against his neighbor. [19] Like a bad tooth and an unsteady foot is confidence in a faithless man in time of trouble. [20] Like one who takes off a garment on a cold day, or like vinegar on soda, is he who sings songs to a troubled heart. [21] If your enemy is hungry, give him food to eat; and if he is thirsty, give him water to drink; [22] For you will heap burning coals on his head, and the Lord will reward you. [23] The north wind brings forth rain, and a backbiting tongue, an angry countenance. [24] It is better to live in a corner of the roof than in a house shared with a contentious woman. [25] Like cold water to a weary soul, so is good news from a distant land. [26] Like a trampled spring and a polluted well is a righteous man who gives way before the wicked. [27] It is not good to eat much honey, nor is it glory to search out one's own glory. [28] Like a city that is broken into and without walls is a man who has no control over his spirit.

PROVERBS 25

PRAYER

ord, it is Your glory and privilege to keep things to Yourself, but the reputation of leaders depends on searching out and discovering things. I also understand that it is better to be invited to a place of honor than to be humiliated by trying to exalt myself. Lord, please help me to know my place today and be content where You have placed me.

Because I choose to be wise today, I won't be in a rush to bring others to court. It is always possible that there may be a good explanation for wrongs that occur. Therefore, I will discuss any conflict privately to avoid humiliation. Don't let me betray another person's confidence; the one who hears it may expose my shameful behavior and damage my reputation. Help me to understand that an evil, gossiping tongue always brings an angry response from others.

Lord, help me speak the right word at the best time. A right word is as valuable as fine jewelry. Is there a good word I can share with someone today? Help me be a faithful friend who refreshes others. Please help me have a gentle tongue. Keep me from the emptiness of falsely boasting about what I give.

I choose to be fair to my friends and neighbors. I want to be sensitive about the number of times I visit with them so I don't overstay my welcome. Keep me from lying about my neighbors. Open my eyes. If I'm putting confidence in an unfaithful friend, show me. Get my attention by making it feel like chewing on a sore tooth or trying to run on a dislocated foot.

Help me today to be sensitive to anyone I encounter who has a heavy heart. I don't want to hurt them more than they already are by trying to cheer them up in the wrong way.

I choose to follow Your advice concerning enemies; that is, if they need something, I'll give it to them if I can. I know that when I do, You will be their judge and reward me for it.

Keep me from contentious people today, Lord. I don't want to be a polluted person, so give me the strength to oppose the wicked. Keep me from the emptiness of promoting myself. I want to be a person of self-control, Lord. Help me to be strong in You.

26

¹ Like snow in summer and like rain in harvest, so honor is not fitting for a fool. ² Like a sparrow in its flitting, like a swallow in its flying, so a curse without cause does not alight. ³ A whip is for the horse, a bridle for the donkey, and a rod for the back of fools. ⁴ Do not answer a fool according to his folly, or you will also be like him. ⁵ Answer a fool as his folly deserves, that he not be wise in his own eyes. ⁶ He cuts off his own feet and drinks violence who sends a message by the hand of a fool. ⁷ Like the legs which are useless to the lame, so is a proverb in the mouth of fools. ⁸ Like one who binds a stone in a sling, so is he who gives honor to a fool. ⁹ Like a thorn which falls into the hand of a drunkard, so is a proverb in the mouth of fools. ¹⁰ Like an archer who wounds everyone, so is he who hires a fool or who hires those who pass by. ¹¹ Like a dog that returns to its vomit is a fool who repeats his folly. ¹² Do you see a man wise in his own eyes? There is more hope for a fool than for him. ¹³ The sluggard says, "There is a lion in the road! A lion is in the open square!" ¹⁴ As the door turns on its hinges, so does the sluggard on his bed. ¹⁵ The sluggard buries his hand in the dish; he is weary of bringing it to his mouth again. ¹⁶ The sluggard is wiser in his own eyes than seven men who can give a discreet answer. ¹⁷ Like one who takes a dog by the ears is he who passes by and meddles with strife not belonging to him.

¹⁸ Like a madman who throws firebrands, arrows and death, ¹⁹ So is the man who deceives his neighbor, and says, "Was I not joking?" ²⁰ For lack of wood the fire goes out, and where there is no whisperer, contention quiets down. ²¹ Like charcoal to hot embers and wood to fire, so is a contentious man to kindle strife. ²² The words of a whisperer are like dainty morsels, and they go down into the innermost parts of the body. ²³ Like an earthen vessel overlaid with silver dross are burning lips and a wicked heart. ²⁴ He who hates disguises it with his lips, but he lays up deceit in his heart. ²⁵ When he speaks graciously, do not believe him, for there are seven abominations in his heart. ²⁶ Though his hatred covers itself with guile, his wickedness will be revealed before the assembly. ²⁷ He who digs a pit will fall into it, and he who rolls a stone, it will come back on him. ²⁸ A lying tongue hates those it crushes, and a flattering mouth works ruin.

PRAYER

hank You for showing me today that there is no honor in being a fool. When responding to people who are foolish, I don't want to act like them. When I do, I become like them. Help me to avoid hiring anyone who is foolish or rebellious. I understand that a fool always repeats his mistakes, which is as pathetic as a dog returning to its own vomit.

It's stupid for me to think I am wiser than anyone else. In fact, there is more hope for a fool than for me when I do that. Please show me today any areas where I think I don't need Your wisdom.

I'm not going to be lazy today, Lord. Convict me for any impudent excuses I have for missed deadlines or laziness on my job. Remove every justification and excuse from my life.

Today, I determine to pass by and avoid the quarrels of others. Thank You for showing me that the benefit of meddling in the fights of others is about the same as grabbing a cat by the tail or a dog by the ears.

Keep me from deceiving my neighbors, even if its only jokingly. I want to help end strife by never being a talebearer or participating in gossip. I can discourage strife by being a peaceful person. Even though others may want to hear what I know, I'm going to keep information to myself. Please close my lips if a touchy subject comes up. Keep me from speaking passionately about things for which I have an ungodly or ulterior motive. Let my words be full of truth today.

Lord, help me recognize those around me who may be full of hatred. Let me see through their deceptive words. Help me to recognize that people who harbor evil in their hearts are full of deceit. When they speak words that seem to be good and truthful, help me to see through their deception. You've shown me that shame fills their hearts, and that their deceitful wickedness will eventually be exposed in front of many people. Please deliver me from their plots so I won't fall into their pit.

27

¹ Do not boast about tomorrow, for you do not know what a day may bring forth. ² Let another praise you, and not your own mouth; a stranger, and not your own lips. ³ A stone is heavy and the sand weighty, but the provocation of a fool is heavier than both of them. ⁴ Wrath is fierce and anger is a flood, but who can stand before jealousy? ⁵ Better is open rebuke than love that is concealed. ⁶ Faithful are the wounds of a friend, but deceitful are the kisses of an enemy. ⁷ A sated man loathes honey, but to a famished man any bitter thing is sweet. ⁸ Like a bird that wanders from her nest, so is a man who wanders from his home. ⁹ Oil and perfume make the heart glad, so a man's counsel is sweet to his friend. ¹⁰ Do not forsake your own friend or your father's friend, and do not go to your brother's house in the day of your calamity; better is a neighbor who is near than a brother far away. ¹¹ Be wise, my son, and make my heart glad, that I may reply to him who reproaches me. ¹² A prudent man sees evil and hides himself, the naive proceed and pay the penalty. ¹³ Take his garment when he becomes surety for a stranger; and for an adulterous woman hold him in pledge. ¹⁴ He who blesses his friend with a loud voice early in the morning, it will be reckoned a curse to him. ¹⁵ A constant dripping on a day of steady rain and a contentious woman are alike; ¹⁶ He who would restrain her restrains

the wind, and grasps oil with his right hand. [17] Iron sharpens iron, so one man sharpens another. [18] He who tends the fig tree will eat its fruit, and he who cares for his master will be honored. [19] As in water face reflects face, so the heart of man reflects man. [20] Sheol and Abaddon are never satisfied, nor are the eyes of man ever satisfied. [21] The crucible is for silver and the furnace for gold, and each is tested by the praise accorded him. [22] Though you pound a fool in a mortar with a pestle along with crushed grain, yet his foolishness will not depart from him. [23] Know well the condition of your flocks, and pay attention to your herds; [24] For riches are not forever, nor does a crown endure to all generations. [25] When the grass disappears, the new growth is seen, and the herbs of the mountains are gathered in, [26] The lambs will be for your clothing, and the goats will bring the price of a field, [27] And there will be goats' milk enough for your food, for the food of your household, and sustenance for your maidens.

PRAYER

ear Lord, is it really possible for me to know what tomorrow will bring? Of course not. But I know You know, so I will trust in You.

If I am to receive any praise today, let it come from someone else and not me. Help me to give praise to others and keep me from being jealous of them. You have said that jealousy can be more dangerous and explosive than anger.

Help me to see that what a true friend does is more trustworthy than anything an enemy says. And when a friend corrects me, it's more valuable than love that's never expressed.

Bring focus to me so I can stay on the right path. I don't want to be a person who won't settle down. Send people into my life who can give me timely advice that refreshes my soul. Help me to never abandon or forsake my own friends or friends of my family. Thank You for all of them, because if problems come my way, it's better to have a close friend than a brother who's far away.

Help me to be wise and bring joy to the heart of my parents today. Keep me from being ignorant, walking blindly, and suffering as a result. Help me to be prudent and foresee impending danger so I can stay away from it.

Stop me from being a quarrelsome person who wearies others like the continuous dripping on a rainy day. Let my relationships be like iron sharpening iron so that we bring out the best in each other.

Help me to always honor my boss at work. In doing so, I know You will reward me. As water reflects my face, so my heart reflects You. Create in me a pure heart, Lord.

Help me to see that each of us is tested by the praise we receive. So, Lord, today I will keep my eyes and ears focused toward You.

Keep me from being a fool and living a foolish life; I know they go hand in hand. I choose to be diligent with everything that I'm responsible for and to watch every interest closely. Do I have some "blind spots" regarding my interests and responsibilities, Lord? Help me to be careful with what I have right now because neither riches nor positions inherited from generations past last forever.

28

¹ The wicked flee when no one is pursuing, but the righteous are bold as a lion. ² By the transgression of a land many are its princes, but by a man of understanding and knowledge, so it endures. ³ A poor man who oppresses the lowly is like a driving rain which leaves no food. ⁴ Those who forsake the law praise the wicked, but those who keep the law strive with them. ⁵ Evil men do not understand justice, but those who seek the LORD understand all things. ⁶ Better is the poor who walks in his integrity than he who is crooked though he be rich. ⁷ He who keeps the law is a discerning son, but he who is a companion of gluttons humiliates his father. ⁸ He who increases his wealth by interest and usury gathers it for him who is gracious to the poor. ⁹ He who turns away his ear from listening to the law, even his prayer is an abomination. ¹⁰ He who leads the upright astray in an evil way will himself fall into his own pit, but the blameless will inherit good. ¹¹ The rich man is wise in his own eyes, but the poor who has understanding sees through him. ¹² When the righteous triumph, there is great glory, but when the wicked rise, men hide themselves. ¹³ He who conceals his transgressions will not prosper, but he who confesses and forsakes them will find compassion. ¹⁴ How blessed is the man who fears always, but he who hardens his heart will fall into calamity. ¹⁵ Like a roaring lion and a rushing bear is a wicked

ruler over a poor people. [16] A leader who is a great oppressor lacks understanding, but he who hates unjust gain will prolong his days. [17] A man who is laden with the guilt of human blood will be a fugitive until death; let no one support him. [18] He who walks blamelessly will be delivered, but he who is crooked will fall all at once. [19] He who tills his land will have plenty of food, but he who follows empty pursuits will have poverty in plenty. [20] A faithful man will abound with blessings, but he who makes haste to be rich will not go unpunished. [21] To show partiality is not good, because for a piece of bread a man will transgress. [22] A man with an evil eye hastens after wealth and does not know that want will come upon him. [23] He who rebukes a man will afterward find more favor than he who flatters with the tongue. [24] He who robs his father or his mother and says, "It is not a transgression," is the companion of a man who destroys. [25] An arrogant man stirs up strife, but he who trusts in the LORD will prosper. [26] He who trusts in his own heart is a fool, but he who walks wisely will be delivered. [27] He who gives to the poor will never want, but he who shuts his eyes will have many curses. [28] When the wicked rise, men hide themselves; but when they perish, the righteous increase.

PRAYER

ord, I see that wicked people spend their lives running from things that aren't after them. But, those who are pure and honest in their dealings can always be as bold as a lion. So teach me, Lord, to be a person of understanding who lives a rock-solid life. Keep me from oppressing the poor in any way. I choose to never turn my back on Your Word or praise the deceitful. Instead, I'll follow Your Word and oppose evil people. I refuse to turn a deaf ear to Your Word, Lord, so my prayers will be pleasing to You.

Lord, let me see today how important it is to have integrity because it is better to have integrity and be poor than to be evil with great riches. As I seek Your counsel, I want to know what is right. Is there any area of my life today where I lack integrity? Is there anything You want me to change or do differently?

Lord, I commit to follow Your Word and to be a discerning person. Lord, protect me from evil people who make themselves richer by cheating others with excessive interest—they eventually lose whatever they gained.

Lord, help me to steer good people away from bad choices today. I want to be blameless and receive a good reward from You. As I prosper, help me to avoid becoming arrogant.

I choose to not cover up my sins today because I won't prosper if I do that. Rather, I confess and abandon them, asking for Your mercy and forgiveness. I will reverence You today and as a result, become a happy, blessed person. Remove from me a hard heart; I don't want the calamity and trouble arrogance produces.

Lead me away from immoral leaders who oppress others. Lord, please help me to never take advantage of those I lead. I choose to hate dishonesty and ill-gotten gain. This decision prolongs my life. Help me to walk blamelessly so I will be kept safe. Deliver me from any perverse ways that could make me fall. I choose to work hard with what I've been given to do. I don't chase after unimportant things or play around; that is the way to keep poverty out of my life.

Lord, I want to be faithful to You and abound with blessings today. Keep me from trying to get rich quick because that will only make me poor. Help me to treat fairly everyone I know. Let me not hesitate when it's right to correct someone. As hard as it may seem at the moment, I know I'll find more favor with that person later than I would if I had flattered him or her. I choose to never steal from my mother or father. If I do that, it is like becoming best friends with a criminal.

Remove from me a proud heart that stirs up strife. Remind me of how nonsensical it is to depend on my own heart. Rather, let me always trust in You and prosper. Send people into my life who are full of wisdom so I will be safe. Finally, Lord, send opportunities my way today to give to the poor, and then I will lack nothing in my life.

By wisdom a house
is built, and by
understanding it
is established; and
by knowledge the
rooms are filled
with all precious
and pleasant riches.

29

¹ A man who hardens his neck after much reproof will suddenly be broken beyond remedy. ² When the righteous increase, the people rejoice, but when a wicked man rules, people groan. ³ A man who loves wisdom makes his father glad, but he who keeps company with harlots wastes his wealth. ⁴ The king gives stability to the land by justice, but a man who takes bribes overthrows it. ⁵ A man who flatters his neighbor is spreading a net for his steps. ⁶ By transgression an evil man is ensnared, but the righteous sings and rejoices. ⁷ The righteous is concerned for the rights of the poor, the wicked does not understand such concern. ⁸ Scorners set a city aflame, but wise men turn away anger. ⁹ When a wise man has a controversy with a foolish man, the foolish man either rages or laughs, and there is no rest. ¹⁰ Men of bloodshed hate the blameless, but the upright are concerned for his life. ¹¹ A fool always loses his temper, but a wise man holds it back. ¹² If a ruler pays attention to falsehood, all his ministers become wicked. ¹³ The poor man and the oppressor have this in common: the Lord gives light to the eyes of both. ¹⁴ If a king judges the poor with truth, his throne will be established forever. ¹⁵ The rod and reproof give wisdom, but a child who gets his own way brings shame to his mother. ¹⁶ When the wicked increase, transgression increases; but the righteous will see their fall. ¹⁷ Correct your son, and he

will give you comfort; he will also delight your soul. ¹⁸ Where there is no vision, the people are unrestrained, but happy is he who keeps the law. ¹⁹ A slave will not be instructed by words alone; for though he understands, there will be no response. ²⁰ Do you see a man who is hasty in his words? There is more hope for a fool than for him. ²¹ He who pampers his slave from childhood will in the end find him to be a son. ²² An angry man stirs up strife, and a hot-tempered man abounds in transgression. ²³ A man's pride will bring him low, but a humble spirit will obtain honor. ²⁴ He who is a partner with a thief hates his own life; he hears the oath but tells nothing. ²⁵ The fear of man brings a snare, but he who trusts in the LORD will be exalted. ²⁶ Many seek the ruler's favor, but justice for man comes from the LORD. ²⁷ An unjust man is abominable to the righteous, and he who is upright in the way is abominable to the wicked.

PRAYER

Lord, I always want to be open for opportunities to improve, even if I have to make changes over and over. I know if I don't, I may be stopped suddenly without getting another chance.

Help me love wisdom every day of my life. By doing so, I will make my father happy and be kept from immoral people who can destroy my life. When I have an opportunity to lead, let me lead honestly while never accepting any kind of bribe. Keep me from flattering people, because when I do, I set a trap for myself. Deliver me from evil people so I won't be tricked by sin. Instead, I choose to celebrate my freedom with singing, rejoicing, and being righteous.

I want to see and care about the poor today. Change my words and thoughts so I don't become a cynic. I choose to never argue with irrational people, then, I can avoid strife and worthless conflicts.

Lord, give me opportunities today to support and encourage people who walk honorably before You. I will always respect honest people.

Teach me to keep from saying everything I feel. Since it is wise to keep my mouth shut and hold back what I want to say, train me to think before I talk. Only hopeless fools speak in haste. When I lead, help me sense when someone is lying. Lying doesn't only affect me, it also hurts those who work with me.

Never let me ignore my children when they need correction because it imparts wisdom. Let me know when punishment is needed, realizing that sometimes discipline doesn't come by words alone. Help me to be consistent in disciplining my children. I know that when I train them correctly, they will bring delight to my soul.

Guide me to become a person of vision and revelation. By doing so, I will live a fruitful life. I receive Your blessings as I keep Your commandments.

Remove anger from me. It stirs up strife and dissension while causing me to commit many sins. And, Lord, keep me from being full of pride today because it limits my growth. Show me how to be humble and gain Your honor.

Keep me from associating with people who steal. Am I in any relationships with people who are dishonest? Lord, expose them to me so I can disassociate myself from them.

I have decided today to be free from the fear of others because this kind of thinking is always an entrapment. Instead, I choose to trust in You and be lifted up. When I desire justice in my life, I turn to You. Real justice only comes from You.

30

¹ The words of Agur the son of Jakeh, the oracle. The man declares to Ithiel, to Ithiel and Ucal: ² Surely I am more stupid than any man, and I do not have the understanding of a man. ³ Neither have I learned wisdom, nor do I have the knowledge of the Holy One. ⁴ Who has ascended into heaven and descended? Who has gathered the wind in His fists? Who has wrapped the waters in His garment? Who has established all the ends of the earth? What is His name or His son's name? Surely you know! ⁵ Every word of God is tested; he is a shield to those who take refuge in Him. ⁶ Do not add to His words or He will reprove you, and you will be proved a liar. ⁷ Two things I asked of You, do not refuse me before I die: ⁸ Keep deception and lies far from me, give me neither poverty nor riches; feed me with the food that is my portion, ⁹ That I not be full and deny You and say, "Who is the LORD?" Or that I not be in want and steal, and profane the name of my God. ¹⁰ Do not slander a slave to his master, or he will curse you and you will be found guilty. ¹¹ There is a kind of man who curses his father and does not bless his mother. ¹² There is a kind who is pure in his own eyes, yet is not washed from his filthiness. ¹³ There is a kind—oh how lofty are his eyes! And his eyelids are raised in arrogance. ¹⁴ There is a kind of man whose teeth are like swords and his jaw teeth like knives, to devour the afflicted from the earth and the needy from among men. ¹⁵ The leech has two daughters, "Give," "Give." There are three things that

will not be satisfied, four that will not say, "Enough": ¹⁶ Sheol, and the barren womb, earth that is never satisfied with water, and fire that never says, "Enough." ¹⁷ The eye that mocks a father and scorns a mother, the ravens of the valley will pick it out, and the young eagles will eat it. ¹⁸ There are three things which are too wonderful for me, four which I do not understand: ¹⁹ The way of an eagle in the sky, the way of a serpent on a rock, the way of a ship in the middle of the sea, and the way of a man with a maid. ²⁰ This is the way of an adulterous woman: she eats and wipes her mouth, and says, "I have done no wrong." ²¹ Under three things the earth quakes, and under four, it cannot bear up: ²² Under a slave when he becomes king, and a fool when he is satisfied with food, ²³ Under an unloved woman when she gets a husband, and a maidservant when she supplants her mistress. ²⁴ Four things are small on the earth, but they are exceedingly wise: ²⁵ The ants are not a strong people, but they prepare their food in the summer; ²⁶ The shephanim are not mighty people, yet they make their houses in the rocks; ²⁷ The locusts have no king, yet all of them go out in ranks; ²⁸ The lizard you may grasp with the hands, yet it is in kings' palaces. ²⁹ There are three things which are stately in their march, even four which are stately when they walk: ³⁰ The lion which is mighty among beasts and does not retreat before any, ³¹ The strutting rooster, the male goat also, and a king when his army is with him. ³² If you have been foolish in exalting yourself or if you have plotted evil, put your hand on your mouth. ³³ For the churning of milk produces butter, and pressing the nose brings forth blood; so the churning of anger produces strife.

PRAYER

ord, I humble myself before Your awesome presence today. I know it is You who ascended and descended from heaven, gathered the wind in Your fists, wrapped up the waters in Your garment, and established all the ends of the earth. So, thank You again today, Lord, for sharing Your wisdom with me.

Your Word is pure and acts as a shield for me when I put my trust in You. I will never add anything to Your Word so You won't have to rebuke me and prove me to be a liar.

Today, I ask two things of You. First, take falsehood and lies far away from me. Second, I ask that You will meet all my needs as You see fit and help me to be content with Your provision. That way, I will never have too much and be tempted to deny You by saying, "Who is the Lord?" Nor will I have too little and be tempted to steal and dishonor Your name.

Lord, keep me from falsely accusing a person to their employer; I want to avoid a liar's judgment. I promise to never curse my father or forget to bless my mother. What are some ways that I can be better to my parents today?

Keep me from seeing myself as pure and faultless despite my many sins. I don't want to be a leach to others by saying, "Give me, give me," yet never feeling satisfied. Keep me from being egotistical and proud. Never let me take advantage of the poor.

Help me to learn wisdom from these four small creatures: the *ant*, that is not strong, but carefully organizes and plans for the future by storing up food in the summertime; the *rock badger*, that is a small animal yet protects itself by living within the rocks; the *locust*, that has no particular leader, yet is effective by working together with the others, advancing orderly in their ranks; and the *lizard*, that is so persevering and industrious it can be found everywhere, even in a king's palace.

Keep me from being foolish by exalting myself or by devising evil. Help me understand that as the churning of milk produces butter and a blow to the nose produces blood, so stirring up anger always causes quarrels. If I am tempted to cause conflict today, lead me to be quiet instead, covering my mouth with my hand.

31

¹ The words of King Lemuel, the oracle which his mother taught him: ² What, O my son? And what, O son of my womb? And what, O son of my vows? ³ Do not give your strength to women, or your ways to that which destroys kings. ⁴ It is not for kings, O Lemuel, it is not for kings to drink wine, or for rulers to desire strong drink, ⁵ For they will drink and forget what is decreed, and pervert the rights of all the afflicted. ⁶ Give strong drink to him who is perishing, and wine to him whose life is bitter. ⁷ Let him drink and forget his poverty and remember his trouble no more. ⁸ Open your mouth for the mute, for the rights of all the unfortunate. ⁹ Open your mouth, judge righteously, and defend the rights of the afflicted and needy. ¹⁰ An excellent wife, who can find? For her worth is far above jewels. ¹¹ The heart of her husband trusts in her, and he will have no lack of gain. ¹² She does him good and not evil all the days of her life. ¹³ She looks for wool and flax and works with her hands in delight. ¹⁴ She is like merchant ships; she brings her food from afar. ¹⁵ She rises also while it is still night and gives food to her household and portions to her maidens. ¹⁶ She considers a field and buys it; from her earnings she plants a vineyard. ¹⁷ She girds herself with strength and makes her arms strong. ¹⁸ She senses that her gain is good; her lamp does not go out at night. ¹⁹ She stretches out her hands to the

distaff, and her hands grasp the spindle. ²⁰ She extends her hand to the poor, and she stretches out her hands to the needy. ²¹ She is not afraid of the snow for her household, for all her household are clothed with scarlet. ²² She makes coverings for herself; her clothing is fine linen and purple. ²³ Her husband is known in the gates, when he sits among the elders of the land. ²⁴ She makes linen garments and sells them, and supplies belts to the tradesmen. ²⁵ Strength and dignity are her clothing, and she smiles at the future. ²⁶ She opens her mouth in wisdom, and the teaching of kindness is on her tongue. ²⁷ She looks well to the ways of her household, and does not eat the bread of idleness. ²⁸ Her children rise up and bless her; her husband also, and he praises her, saying: ²⁹ "Many daughters have done nobly, but you excel them all." ³⁰ Charm is deceitful and beauty is vain, but a woman who fears the Lord, she shall be praised. ³¹ Give her the product of her hands, and let her works praise her in the gates.

proverbs 31

PRAYER

~for women~

Lord, thank You for helping me to be a moral woman, full of godly purpose. And thank You for showing me that virtue is more precious than fine gems.

Please keep me from being a woman who is promiscuous in any way, who takes away the strength of men and destroys leaders. Let me not make a fool of myself by drinking alcohol, thereby disqualifying myself from helping those who are oppressed. Instead, help me to defend those who can't help themselves. Help me speak out for justice and stand up for the poor.

Help me to be a woman that my (future) husband's heart can safely trust, a person in whom he can have full confidence. Show him how to treat me with respect and dignity, and teach me how to be good to him. Is there anything special that I can do today for my (future) husband?

In order to care for my family, help me to rise early every day. I choose to be wise with my purchases, using profits wisely and saving in order to gain even more. Open my eyes to see the best possible bargains. Give me strength and willingness to work into the night when a project requires it. Help me to be a diligent, energetic worker, well able to do whatever tasks I need to perform every day. I want to work skillfully, eagerly, and willingly with my hands.

Help me to open my arms to the poor and my hands to the needy. Assist me in thinking ahead to prepare my household for bad weather so that everyone is clothed appropriately.

Lord, help me to understand that by being virtuous I will be a positive reflection on my husband. Show me how my actions can bring him respect and favor in our community. Help me to be a person of strength and honor.

And finally, Lord, help me to fearlessly look forward to the future. Fill my mouth with wisdom and my tongue with words of kindness. Lead me to be watchful about everything that goes on in my house. Through the wisdom You give, may my children greet me with blessing and even praise me. Help me to see that charm and beauty can be deceitful, but that a woman who respects You will be honored and praised.

PROVERBS 31

PRAYER

~FOR MEN~

Lord, I thank You that You are faithful to show me potential pitfalls in my life. Help me not to give my strength away to evil, promiscuous women who seek to destroy leaders. Thank You for reminding me of the foolishness of drinking alcohol. I want to help the oppressed, and alcohol only clouds my mind. Help me always to defend those who can't help themselves. Help me to speak out for justice and to stand up for the poor.

Your wisdom shows me the character of a truly virtuous woman, Lord. Thank You for my (future) virtuous wife. Because of Your wisdom, I understand that her worth is far more valuable than precious gems. As her (future) husband, my heart can safely trust her. I can have full confidence in her and treasure her. I thank You that she is good and not evil to me and pray that she will remain the same throughout her life. Help her to work skillfully, eagerly, and willingly with her hands, meeting the needs of our family. Is there anything special I can do for my (future) wife today? Please show me, Lord.

I pray that my virtuous (future) wife will be wise with her purchases and will use the profits and savings to produce even more. May she be a diligent and energetic worker, well able to do whatever tasks she needs to perform. Help her to be on the lookout for the best possible bargains. Thank You that she opens her arms to the poor and reaches out her hands to the needy. Assist her in thinking ahead and preparing our entire household for bad weather by seeing that everyone is clothed appropriately.

Through her virtue, I will gain respect and favor in my community. Thank You that due to her strength and honor, she will stand out like a beautiful dress. May she not be afraid of the future but confidently look forward to it. Let me hear her wisdom and relax in her beautiful kindness.

Help my (future) wife to be careful about everything that goes on throughout our household and to be industrious. May our children call her blessed, and let me praise her, saying, "Many other women have done good things, but you surpass them all. You are the best one!"

Help me to see that charm is deceitful and beauty doesn't last, but a woman who respects God will be praised. Show me how to reward her often for what she has done. Let others praise my precious (future) wife for her godly example.

Proverbs
Principles For:

ACHIEVEMENT

By wisdom a house is built, and by
understanding it is established.

PROVERBS 24:3

Opportunity is all around you. What matters is where you put your focus. Ask God this question every day: "Where should my focus be?" Where you focus your attention, you create strength and momentum.

There is always a heavy demand for fresh mediocrity—don't give in to it. Instead, be only satisfied with the very best. For when you are delivering your very best, that is when you will feel most successful. Your character is your destiny. Never sell your principles for popularity or you'll find yourself bankrupt in the worst way. Dare to be true to the best you know.

ADVICE

Where there is no guidance the people fall, but in
abundance of counselors there is victory.

PROVERBS 11:14

There are two quick ways to disaster: taking nobody's advice and taking everybody's advice. Learn to say no to the good so you can say yes to the best. A. P. Goethe says there are three qualifications for success: "1) A big waste basket—you must know what to eliminate; 2) It is important to know what to preserve; 3) It is important to know when to say no, for developing the power to say no gives us the capacity to say yes."

ANGER

He who is slow to anger is better than the mighty, and
he who rules his spirit, than he who captures a city.

PROVERBS 16:32

The best time for you to hold your tongue is the time you feel you *must* say something or burst. You'll never be hurt by anything you didn't say. Silence is the ultimate weapon of power; it's also one of the hardest arguments to dispute.

Take a tip from nature—your ears aren't made to shut, but your mouth is! When an argument flares up, the wise man quenches it with silence. Sometimes you have to be quiet to be heard. It's when the fish opens his mouth that he gets caught.

CHARACTER

He who walks in integrity walks securely, but he who perverts his ways will be found out.

PROVERBS 10:9

Excellence measures a man by the height of his ideals, the breadth of his compassion, the depth of his convictions, and the length of his persistence. People will always determine your character by observing what you stand for, fall for, and lie for.

"Watch your actions; they become habits. Watch your habits; they become character. Watch your character; it becomes your destiny" (Frank Outlaw).

COMPASSION

He who oppresses the poor taunts his Maker, but he who is gracious to the needy honors Him.

PROVERBS 14:31

"Unless life is lived for others, it is not worthwhile" (Mother Teresa). "A self-centered life is totally empty, while an empty life allows room for God" (Tom Haggai). A good way to forget your troubles is to help others out of their troubles.

Whatever we praise, we increase. There is no investment you can make that will pay you so well as the effort to scatter sunshine and compassion into others throughout your journey.

CONCEIT

Do you see a man wise in his own eyes? There is more hope for a fool than for him.

PROVERBS 26:12

Remember, if you try to go it alone, the fence that shuts others out, shuts you in. "God sends no one away except those who are full of themselves" (D. L. Moody). The man who only works by himself and for himself is likely to be corrupted by the company he keeps.

The man who believes in nothing but himself lives in a very small world—one in which few will want to enter. The man who sings his own praises may have the right tune but the wrong words. A conceited person never gets anywhere because he thinks he's already there.

DILIGENCE

Go to the ant, O sluggard, observe her ways and be wise.

One of the Devil's strategies to get you to fail is for you to procrastinate. Realize that now is the best time to be alive and productive. If you want to make an easy job seem difficult, just keep putting off doing it. "A duty dodged is like a debt unpaid; it is only deferred and we must come back and settle the account at last" (Joseph Newton).

Nothing is so fatiguing as the eternal hanging-on of an uncompleted task. When you run in place everyone will pass you by. Do today what you want to postpone until tomorrow.

DIRECTION

The mind of man plans his way, but the Lord directs his steps.

Here is a key to life...ask God to direct your steps. He will! Discover God's direction and purpose for your life. Successful lives are motivated by dynamic purpose. God can only bless your plan and direct you in accomplishing it if you have one. Strong convictions precede great actions.

The man who has no direction is the slave of his circumstances. If your method is hit or miss, you'll usually miss. "If you're not sure where you are going, you'll probably end up someplace else" (Robert F. Mager).

DISCIPLINE

He who neglects discipline despises himself, but he who listens to reproof acquires understanding.

PROVERBS 15:32

"You will never be the person you can be if pressure, tension, and discipline are taken out of your life" (James Bilkey). Refuse to let yourself become discouraged by temporary setbacks. If you are beginning to encounter some hard bumps, don't worry. At least you are out of a rut. Circumstances are not your master.

You can always measure a person by the amount of opposition it takes to discourage him. When the water starts to rise, you can too.

FAITH

*The fear of man brings a snare, but he who
trusts in the Lord will be exalted.*

PROVERBS 29:25

We live by faith or we don't live at all. What's needed is more people who specialize in the impossible. This year's success was last year's impossibility. "Faith is not trying to believe something regardless of the evidence. Faith is daring to do something regardless of the consequence" (Sherwood Eddy).

Never be afraid to do what God has directed you to do. You do not tap the resources of God until you attempt the impossible. Risk is part of God's plan. Unless it involves faith, it's not worthy of being called God's direction.

FRIENDS

*He who walks with wise men will be wise, but
the companion of fools will suffer harm.*

PROVERBS 13:20

Who you choose to be your closest friends or associates is one of the most important decisions you will make during the course of your life.

I've found that the best friends are those who bring out the best in you, and a real good friend is someone who knows all about you and likes you anyway. A true friend is someone who is there for you when they'd rather be somewhere else. I believe that we should keep our friendships in constant repair. Instead of just loving our enemies, we should also treat our friends better.

GOSSIP

For lack of wood the fire goes out, and where there is no whisperer, contention quiets down.

PROVERBS 26:20

Talk is cheap because supply exceeds demand. "As you go through life, you're going to have many opportunities to keep your mouth shut. Take advantage of all of them" (West Virginia Gazette). There must have been some reason God made our ears to stay open and our mouths to shut. Your ears will never get you in trouble.

Don't be known as a person whose only words are negative. Contrary to what you may have heard, talk is not cheap. Talk is powerful! What we say affects what we get from others and what others get from us.

GUIDANCE

*For the commandment is a lamp and the teaching is
light; and reproofs for discipline are the way of life.*

PROVERBS 6:23

What good is aim if you don't know when to pull the trig-
ger? God's a God of timing *and* direction. He wants us to
know what to do and when to do it. "[His] word is a lamp to
my feet and a light to my path" (Psalm 119:105). The lamp
illuminates things we are dealing with close at hand. The
light on our path enlightens our future direction.

If you are facing the right direction, just keep on walking.
Your success has less to do with speed, but more to do with
doing the right thing at the right time. His Word illuminates
the way.

HUMILITY

*A prudent man sees evil and hides himself,
the naive proceed and pay the penalty.*

PROVERBS 27:12

I like what Dwight L. Moody said: "Be humble or you'll
stumble." There are two types of people in the world: those

who come into a room and say, "Here I am!" and those who come in and say, "Ah, there you are!"

How do you know a good person? They think of others before themselves. A good person makes others better. They find happiness by helping others find it.

KNOWLEDGE

The mind of the prudent acquires knowledge,
and the ear of the wise seeks knowledge.

PROVERBS 18:15

Stay hungry for right knowledge. Don't look for *an* answer to your problem; look for *many* answers, then choose the best one. The person who succeeds is the one who does more than is necessary—and continues doing it. "The difference between ordinary and extraordinary is that little extra" (Zig Ziglar).

The deeper we go in God, the deeper He goes in us. "A wise man will hear and increase in learning" (Proverbs 1:5). If you're satisfied with what's good, you'll never have what's best. "It's what you learn after you know it all that counts" (John Wooden).

LAZINESS

Poor is he who works with a negligent hand,
but the hand of the diligent makes rich.

PROVERBS 10:4

Hardly anything is more dangerous to a person's character than having nothing to do and plenty of time in which to do it. Two things rob people of their peace of mind: work unfinished and work not yet begun.

The test of a person lies in action. No one ever stumbled onto something big while sitting down. A famous anonymous poem states, "Sitting still and wishing makes no person great, the good Lord sends the fishing, but you must dig the bait."

LOVE

Hatred stirs up strife, but love covers all transgressions.

PROVERBS 10:12

"What force is more potent than love?" (Igor Stravinsky). Love is the most important ingredient of success. Without it your life will echo with emptiness. Jesus said, "By this shall all men know that ye are my disciples, if ye have love one to another" (John 13:35 KJV).

Kindness has converted more sinners than zeal, eloquence, or learning. Love people more than they deserve. "You will find as you look back upon your life that the moments when you have really lived, are the moments when you have done things in a spirit of love" (Henry Drummond).

MOTIVATION

Every man's way is right in his own eyes,
but the Lord weighs the heart.

PROVERBS 21:2

One of the most frequent prayers I pray is based on the Scripture found in Psalm 51:10. I've found that this prayer has been a key in my life. "Create in me a clean heart, O God, and renew a steadfast spirit within me." There is a supernatural confidence, expectancy, and peace that comes when we have a clean heart and a right spirit before the Father.

A pure heart will bring increased strength to your life. Be used for a mighty purpose. Dare to do what's right for you. Something significant always happens when our hearts are wholly submitted to Him.

PATIENCE

A faithful man will abound with blessings, but he who makes haste to be rich will not go unpunished.

PROVERBS 28:20

The road to success runs uphill so don't expect to break any speed records. Impatience is costly. Your greatest mistakes will happen because of impatience. Most people fail simply because they're impatient and cannot join the beginning with the end. You need to keep on patiently doing God's will if you want Him to do for you all that He has promised.

It's more important to know where you're going, than to see how fast you can get there. "Impatient people always get there too late" (Jean Dutourd). Impatience is one big "get-ahead-ache."

PEACE

When a man's ways are pleasing to the Lord, he
makes even his enemies to be at peace with him.

PROVERBS 16:7

You're not free until you've been made captive by God's supreme plan for your life. In His will is our peace. Only those who are bound to Christ are truly free.

Peace is the result of a deliberate decision, an adjustment of your life to the will of God. "Don't worry about anything; instead, pray about everything. Tell God what you need, and thank him for all he has done. Then you will experience God's peace, which exceeds anything we can understand. His peace will guard your hearts and minds as you live in Christ Jesus." (Philippians 4:6–7 NLT).

PERSISTENCE

Do you see a man skilled in his work? He will stand
before kings; he will not stand before obscure men.

PROVERBS 22:29

"The nose of a bulldog is slanted backwards so he can continue to breathe without letting go" (Winston Churchill). Persistent people begin their success where most others quit.

One person with commitment, persistence, and endurance will accomplish more than a thousand people with interest alone.

The more diligently we work, the harder it is to quit. Persistence is a habit—so is quitting. Many people eagerly fight "the good fight of faith," but they forget to add patience, persistence, and endurance to their enthusiasm. Josh Billings said, "Consider the postage stamp. Its usefulness consists of the ability to stick to something until it gets there." You and I should be known as "postage stamp" Christians.

PRIDE

*Pride goes before destruction, and a
haughty spirit before stumbling.*

PROVERBS 16:18

Thinking too often about yourself shrinks your world. Thinking about others enlarges it. There really is no such thing as a "self-made man." But how many people proudly proclaim "I did it all myself?" We are conditioned to think primarily about ourselves. That is why 97 percent of all people will write their own names when they are offered a new pen to try.

Since the majority of our unhappiness comes from thinking about ourselves, maybe it is time to stop. It has been proven that you can succeed best and quickest by helping others succeed.

When its "all about you," you'll find yourself bound on the north, south, east, and west by just yourself. With no support, you are lonely and unprotected. No person is more cheated than a prideful person.

RIGHTEOUSNESS

But the path of the righteous is like the light of dawn, that shines brighter and brighter until the full day.

PROVERBS 4:18

Do what's right. "I say, let the Holy Spirit guide your lives. Then you won't be doing what your sinful nature craves." (Galatians 5:16 NLT). Human excellence means nothing unless it works with the consent of God. Walking in righteousness with God's help you can be better than yourself.

TEMPTATION

Do not enter the path of the wicked and do not proceed in the way of evil men.

PROVERBS 4:14

Yes and *no* are the two most important words you will ever say. How and when you say them affects your entire future. There is power in the word *no*. *No* is an anointed word that can break the yoke of overcommitment and weakness. Saying *no* can free you from any temptation. Saying *no* to wrong things can mean saying *yes* to God's priorities in your life.

No one can be caught in a place they do not visit. Evil unchecked, grows. Evil tolerated, poisons you and all those you care about. Keep true, never be ashamed of doing right; decide on what you know is right and stick to it.

TRUST

Trust in the Lord with all your heart and do not lean on your own understanding. In all your ways acknowledge Him, and He will make your paths straight.

PROVERBS 3:5-6

You may trust the Lord too little, but you can never trust Him too much. When you leave God out, you'll find yourself without any invisible means of support. Nothing great has ever been achieved except by those who dared believe that God inside them was superior to circumstance. The way each day will look to you all starts with whom you're looking to. Look to God. Never undertake anything for which you wouldn't have the conviction to ask the blessing of heaven. A small man stands on others. A great man stands on God.

VISION

Where there is no vision, the people are unrestrained,
but happy is he who keeps the law.

PROVERBS 29:18

A shallow thinker seldom makes a deep impression. We act, or fail to act, not because of *will*, as is so commonly believed, but because of *vision*. Only one who sees the invisible can do the impossible.

Dissatisfaction and discouragement aren't a result of the absence of things, but the absence of vision. Not being a person of imagination causes your life to be less than it was intended to be.

A dream is the most exciting thing there is. Vision adds value to everything. A single idea—the sudden flash of any thought—may be worth a million dollars, change a nation, or help save a soul.

WISDOM

*The beginning of wisdom is: Acquire wisdom; and
with all your acquiring, get understanding.*

PROVERBS 4:7

When you have heard God's voice, you have heard His
wisdom. Thank God for His powerful wisdom. It forces a pas-
sage through the strongest barriers.

An old adage says, "He who knows nothing doubts nothing." In addition, he who knows has a solid basis for his belief.
Wisdom is seeing everything from God's perspective. Knowing
when and how to use the knowledge comes from the Lord.

WORDS

*A man has joy in an apt answer, and
how delightful is a timely word!*

PROVERBS 15:23

Words are like nitroglycerine: They can blow up bridges
or heal hearts. Just to see how it feels for the next twenty-
four hours, refrain from saying anything bad about anybody
or anything. "The difference between the right word and the
almost right word is the difference between lightning and the

lightning bug," said Mark Twain. It's true, "Death and life are in the power of the tongue" (Proverbs 18:21).

You can tell more about a person by what he says about others than you can by what others say about him. Out of the abundance of the heart, the mouth speaks. Our words are seeds planted into others lives.

He who trusts
in the Lord will
be exalted.

ABOUT THE AUTHOR

John Mason is a national best-selling author, minister, executive coach, and noted speaker. He's the founder and president of Insight International, an organization dedicated to helping people reach their dreams and fulfill their God-given destinies.

He has authored fourteen books including *An Enemy Called Average, You're Born an Original—Don't Die a Copy, Let Go of Whatever Makes You Stop,* and *Know Your Limits—Then Ignore Them,* which have sold over 1.4 million copies and been translated into thirty-five languages. His books are widely respected as a source of godly wisdom, scriptural motivation, and practical principles. His writings have been published in *Reader's Digest* along with numerous other national publications.

Known for his quick wit, powerful thoughts, and insightful ideas, he is a popular speaker across the United States and around the world. John and his wife, Linda, have four children: Michelle, Greg, Michael, and David. They reside in Tulsa, Oklahoma.

YOU CAN CONTACT HIM AT:

John Mason
P.O. Box 54996
Tulsa, OK 74155
www.freshword.com
contact@freshword.com

A FINAL WORD

Webster's New World Dictionary defines "wisdom" as demonstrating "good judgment." I pray that as you journey through each day, the quality of your life will be enhanced as a result of your good judgment.

Take *Proverbs Prayers* everywhere you go. Allow the Word of God to speak wisdom into your life. Ask God to help you make daily decisions that reflect good judgment.

You'll soon discover that His wisdom breaks chains, unlocks doors, and illuminates your path!